Publisher's Note

The book descriptions we ask booksellers to display prominently warn that the book may have numerous typos, missing text, images and indexes.

We scanned this book using character recognition software that includes an automated spell check. Our software is 99 percent accurate if the book is in good condition. However, we do understand that even one percent can be a very annoying number of typos! And sometimes all or part of a page is missing from our copy of a book. Or the paper may be so discolored from age that you can no longer read the type. Please accept our sincere apologies.

After we re-typeset and design a book, the page numbers change so the old index and table of contents no longer work. Therefore, we often remove them.

We would like to manually proof read and fix the typos and indexes, manually scan and add any illustrations, and track down another copy of the book to add any missing text. But our books sell so few copies, you would have to pay up to a thousand dollars for the book as a result.

Therefore, whenever possible, we let our customers download a free copy of the original typo-free scanned book. Simply enter the barcode number from the back cover of the paperback in the Free Book form at www.general-books. net. You may also qualify for a free trial membership in our book club to download up to four books for free. Simply enter the barcode number from the back cover onto the membership form on the same page. The book club entitles you to select from more than a million books at no additional charge. Simply enter the title or subject onto the search form to find the books.

If you have any questions, could you please be so kind as to consult our Frequently Asked Questions page at www. general-books.net/faqs.cfm? You are also welcome to contact us there.

General Books LLC®, Memphis, USA, 2012. ISBN: 9781154153484.

❄ ❄ ❄ ❄ ❄ ❄ ❄ ❄

PREFACE.

In December, 1901, William Walker Atkinson in assuming the editorship of the popular magazine New Thought, introduced himself to the readers of that periodical in a memorable article. That article contained a clear, ringing, forceful statement of his individual creed, than which nothing can afford a deeper insight into the character and inner self of the man whose name appears as author of this book. It is the crystallized expression of the world-principles, the truths, which his writings seek to illuminate, and in my opinion should be read by every student of his works, as the key to the philosophy he teaches.

For this reason there has been prefixed to this, his latest book, under the title "My Working Creed," the most vital of the fundamental beliefs enunciated by Mr. Atkinson in that famous introductory statement of 1901. None can read the recurring, ringing "I BELIEVE" of this author, without feeling an answering thrill of exaltation and power. To those who read this book I would say, imbue yourself thoroughly with the broad and beautiful spirit of those few preliminary paragraphs that you may pass on understandingly to the perusal of the teachings which follow.

Those who have an opportunity to refer to the article from which this Creed is taken, should do so. It tells of the work, the material success, followed by over-strain, physical and mental breakdown and financial disaster, which marked the earlier years of William Walker Atkinson. It shows how he came to know what he now holds to be The Truth, and how, in his own life, he has demonstrated its value. For from mental and physical wreck and financial ruin, he wrought through its principles, perfect health, mental vigor and material prosperity.

Mr. Atkinson, during the many years

of his connection with the magazine, New Thought, built for himself an enduring place in the hearts of its readers. For four years his literary work was confined to its pages (including in addition, three books for its publishers), and article after article of wonderful strength and vital force flowed from his pen. During this time several

Included In "New Thought Annual for 1902" published by The New Thought Publishing Co.

series of "lessons" appeared, under varying titles, in regard to the application of the Law of Attraction in the Thought World, lessons which created a sensation and exerted a wonderful in-/ fluence upon the lives of those who applied their principles. They were written in Mr. Atkinson's own sparkling, intimate style, teeming with thought, force, energy, fire, but shorn of all atmosphere of the study, all attempt at "fine writing," polished periods or dignified metaphor, and all affectation or assumption of superior learning. One of Mr. Atkinson's cardinal principles is "Stand on your own feet," and he deprecates any attempt to read infallibility into his writings. For this reason we have again prefaced the present work with a "Foreword" in which he seeks to instill into all students of New Thought, whether as expressed in his writings or in those of others,—the quality of self-dependence. A reading of this Foreword will give the student a clear idea of the attitude of mind in which Mr. Atkinson thinks this and all other individual interpret-tions of life should be approached.

With "My Working Creed" and the "Foreword" as guides, the present reader should enter upon Thought Vibration, the book proper, in a spirit calculated to extract the greatest possible value.

Thought Vibration embraces two series of the vital lessons mentioned above, with some additional articles by Mr. Atkinson following out the same line of teaching. The order of the lessons has been somewhat changed in the combination; and for further continuity and clearness, new lesson titles in the form of chapter headings have been selected. The publishers have preferred to retain the familiar unstudied style of the lessons, as originally written, rather than to subject the articles to the literary revision by the author which usually precedes publication in book form. They contend that Mr. Atkinson's mightiest influence, his greatest strength and power, lies in his simple, straightforward, and at times even colloquial language—the kind which "even my little son can understand," as wrote in gratitude one earnest student. It is such writing that the world needs,—writing which can be read and apprehended by the "little sons" of the world, whether known as children or as men. There is a great deal of so-called "fine writing" on New Thought subjects, beautiful sentences full of high, though sometimes misty thought; but this world needs common, practical, everyday application of this thought. Where there is one reader for the literary masterpiece, there are a hundred readers (plus even that other one), for the book written as a keen, live, human man *talks,* and written about the difficulties, the problems, the possibilities of the average citizen of the world.

This is a truth Mr. Atkinson has mastered, and it is with intention he casts from him the restrictions of an academic style. He speaks, always, not in dignified tones to "the public," but in the language of a friend to YOU. It can be said of him in praise, as of another before him: *"The common people heard 'him gladly!"*—the highest, most enduring tribute that can be paid to a leader of men.

Recognition is due to Louise Radford Wells for the revision of the proofs of this book, the selection of its title and chapter headings, and the ordered arrangement of the lessons.

Franklin L. Berry, Editor of *New Thought. June 15, ipo6 Chicago, Illinois.* works on the sub-conscious plane along the line of the ruling passion or desire—Scattering thoughtforce—Getting out of the current of attraction—

My personal experience—"Love" at the bottom of the whole of life—The so-called "chemical affinities"—Desire a manifestation of this Universal Life Love.

CHAPTER XIV

The Great Dynamic Forces

The difference between the successful strong men and the unsuccessful weak men—Energy and Invincible Determination—Energy not rare—Wasted nerve-force—The Human Will—A great dynamic force—The people who have "arrived"—Are they "ordinary," after all?—Made of the stuff of those about them—Wherein does their greatness lief—Belief in themselves—The right use of material—The "trick" of greatness—The good things locked up in your mind—The inexhaustible supply.

CHAPTER XV

Claiming Your Own

Nothing too good for you—Your direct inheritance— Great things lost for want of asking—The Law takes you in earnest—You are a manifestation of the Whole Thing—You must first awaken to a realization that you are merely asking for "your own"—The Law will do its work—The hypnotism of '' humility''—The great things in the Cosmos which await your coming of age—The playthings of life —Our game-tasks—The difference between the Master of Circumstances and the Slave of Circumstances.

CHAPTER XVI

Law, Not Chance

The Attractive Power of Thought—"A matter of luck"—A magnificent illustration of the Law of Attraction—A strong belief as efficacious as a strong wish—The man who "gets there"—The man who fails—No such thing as Chance—Law everywhere—Plan and purpose; cause and effect— The right vibrations—Getting into the current.

FOREWORD.

I am in receipt of a letter from an earnest student of New Thought, who writes me that he is endeavoring to put into practice the teachings for which I stand. That is all right—I think he will get some good out of the practice (I

know that *I do).* But here is where the trouble comes in—he goes on to say that he is "a faithful disciple" of mine, and is content to "sit at the feet of the Teacher." Now, if you will pardon the slang, I must say that such talk "makes me tired." I wish no "disciples"—disciples are mere parrots repeating what one says—mere human sheep trotting along after some conceited old bell-wether. I do not wish to pose as a bell-wether, nor do I wish a flock of human sheep trotting after me. I want everyone of my fellow students of Mental Science to be his own bell-wether. I like comradeship and mutual help—the help of interdependence. But I don't like this talk of master and disciple—of leader and follower—this talk and idea of dependence.

As for sitting at any one's feet, the idea arouses all the spirit of independence within me. I don't want to sit at any one's feet—and I don't want any one to sit at mine. I am willing, and often glad, to listen to some teacher and to pick from his teachings such bits of truth as my mind is ready to receive. I am willing to say "I don't know," and to accept from others that which appeals to me as truth; not because the other says that it is truth, but because my mind recognizes it as such. I take my own wherever I find it, because I recognize it as mine. I know that all students and teachers get their knowledge from the only source of supply—they can't get it from anywhere else. And if some other fellow happens to see a particular bit of truth before I do, I gladly accept a portion of it from his hands, be he king or beggar; while if I happen to see the thing first, I will gladly share it with all who are ready for it, and who may want it, without feeling that I am a "leader," or "teacher," or that they are "followers" or "disciples." We are all fellow students—that's all. I recognize no man as my master—and I spurn the person who would call me "Master," if there be any so foolish. This feet-sitting talk makes me very, very weary,

I am fully aware that certain teachers convey the idea that they are chosen mouthpieces of the Infinite, and that all true teachings must bear their hallmark. And I also know the fanatical devotion and bigotry that many of the followers of such teachers manifest. But this is all child's play. The teachers sooner or later will be brought up against good hard stone walls, and their heads will be bruised until they realize "just where they are at." And the "disciples" will have some individuality knocked into them later on, and will be made to stand upon their own feet, by reason of the props being knocked from under them. The New Thought aims at making individuals, not at converting people into droves of sheep, following the tinkle of the bell of some conceited old bell-wether, who imagines that he is the Whole Thing.

The growing soul must realize that it has within itself all that it requires. It may gladly accept from others suggestions, advice, bits of knowledge, and the like, as it goes along—the soul itself being the only judge of what it requires at each particular stage. But, in the end, it must do its own work, and must stand on its own feet. All the teachings in the world will not help you, unless you take hold of the matter yourself and work out your own salvation. You cannot get true mental or spiritual teaching by simply paying so much for a course of lessons, and doing nothing yourself. You must bring something to the teacher before you can take anything away. You must work up to an understanding before the teachings of another will do you any good.

The teacher may make a suggestion that will open up a line of thought for you, or he may point out a way that has proved of value to him; and thus save you much time and trouble. But you must do the real work yourself.

A teacher may be so filled with the truth that he will overflow, and you will get some of the overflow. I believe that truth is "catching." But even so, unless you make that truth your own by living it out, and applying it to your needs, it will do you no good. And so long as you are content to "sit at his feet," and do the "disciple" act, you will not grow one inch. You will be merely a reflection of the teacher, instead of being an individual.

We need a jogging up on this point every once in a while, "lest we forget." It is so easy to have your thoughts predigested for you by some teacher or writer—so easy to receive your teaching in capsules. It is so nice to be able to sit down and swallow the tabloid that the teacher or writer kindly has prepared for you, and imagine that you are getting the real thing. But I tell you, friends—*it won't do the work.* Imbibe all the teachings you please, but you have got to get down to business yourself. You can't give some one else a power of attorney to do the work in your place. Life accepts no substitutes—you must step out yourself. It is mighty easy—this idea of paying so much, in time or money, to some teacher or writer, and then sneaking into the Kingdom of Heaven holding on to his skirts— but it won't work. You've got to do some hustling on your own account, and don't you make any mistake about this fact.

Many of you are running around after teachers, preachers, prophets, seers, "illuminated souls," and what not, expecting that your little fee for courses of lessons, private teachings, and all the rest, is going to land you right up in the front rank. Don't you believe a word of it. You've got to go through the motions yourself, before you will attain anything. You can't sneak in that way—it won't work. I look around me and see many of these poor creatures "sitting at the feet" of some one or other, sinking their individuality in that of the teacher, and not daring to think an original thought—lest it conflict with some notion of their "Master." These good souls are so full of the teaching they are imbibing, they will repeat it by the yard, phrase after phrase, like a well-trained parrot. But they don't understand a bit of it. They are like the moon which shines by reason of the reflection of the sun's rays, and has no light or heat of its own. The talk of these "disciples" and "sitters-at-the-feet" is nothing but moonshine—mere reflected light. Moons are dead, cold things—no light—no heat —no fire—no energy. Dead, dead, dead—cold, barren and "played-out." Stop this moon business and build yourself up into a Sun. You have it in you—manifest it. Start yourself in motion, and manifest Life. Don't suppose that you must be able to solve all the Riddles of the Universe before you can do anything. Never mind about those riddles, just you get down to the task that lies ahead of you, and throw into it some of that Great Life Principle that is within you waiting for a chance to manifest itself. Don't make the mistake of supposing that this or that teacher has solved the Great Riddle. If he says he has, he is only bluffing and whistling to keep up courage. He may have found a good-sized chunk of the truth, and if he is willing to pass you a bit of it, all right, but he hasn't the Whole Thing, by a mighty sight. The Whole Thing isn't placing itself in the exclusive control of any little bit of itself. No one has a monopoly of knowing—a corner on the Truth. It is yours as much as anybody's—but you must dig for it.

Don't bother about the theories, or the unsolvable riddles—just get down to business and begin to Live. Sometimes I amuse myself by reading some of the theories and "explanations" of those who think that they have hold of the Whole Thing. After I get through with the theories of one "dead-sure" chap, I take up the directly opposite theories of another fellow who considers himself the special mouthpiece of the Absolute. Whew! it's a great brain-shaker. If you're not careful you will find yourself being served a nice dish of scrambled brains. When I get sort of "stewed-up" over such things I go out into the sun and fall back on the "Laughing Philosophy," which soon brings me around all right. Nothing will puncture these bubbles so quickly as a good dose of Laughter. Laughter is the only thing that keeps the race from madness. The sense of humor is God's best gift to Man. Try it the next time you get "stewed up" with "high statements," "basic truths," "axiomatic principles." Beware of any teachings that will not stand the test of the sunny out-of-doors, and the application of the Laughing Philosophy. Shun the teachings that require a pursed-up mouth, and a strained, preternaturally sober face. Have nothing to do with teachings that require a dim, dark, sunless room to be absorbed in— beware of teachings and doctrines that bear the musty smell of the cell upon them. Carry out into the sun the teachings that are offered you, and see whether or not they fade—apply the chemical of laughter, and ascertain whether the stuff bleaches. Remember this test when you are perplexed or worried over some strange theory or doctrine—no matter from whence it comes. If any one tells you that which will not bear the test— discard the teaching, for it is spurious in that event. Try this on my writings along with the others.

Stop being moons. Stop living by reflected light. Get into action and convert yourself into a living sun. You can do it. It is within your power. Every human soul contains within it the elements of the Sun—get to work and express yourself. Stiffen up your backbone and hold your head erect. Don't be afraid to say "I am IT."

This is a straight-from-the-shoulder talk. Don't tell me that you are "disciples" of mine—I disown you; I refuse to have disciples. Don't try to "sit at my feet"—if you do, I will use my feet to push you off the platform. I need room to swing my feet about and don't want people sitting there. But if you wish to call me "Brother," or "Fellow Student," or "Schoolmate in the Kindergarten of God," I will be glad to have you do so. That's all we are, after all—little babes tugging away at the breast of the Absolute.

William Walker Atkinson. MY WORKING CREED.

I believe that the mind of Man contains the greatest of all forces—that Thought is one of the greatest manifestations of energy. I believe that the man who understands the use of Thought-force can make of himself practically what he will. I believe that not only is one's body subject to the control of the mind, but that, also, one may change environment, "luck," *circumstances, by positive thought taking the place of negative. I know that the "I Can and I Will" attitude will carry one forward to Success that will seem miraculous to the man on the "I Can't" plane. I believe that "thoughts are things," and that the Law of Attraction in the thought world will draw to one just what he desires or fears. I believe in the gospel of work—in "hustling." I believe in the I DO, as well as the I AM. I know that the man who will take advantage of the Power of the Mind, and who will manifest that power in action, will go forward to Success as surely and as steadily as the arrow from the bow of the skilled archer. I believe in the Brotherhood of Man. I believe in being Kind. I believe in everyone minding his own business —and allowing everyone else the same privilege.. I believe that we have no right to condemn— "let him who is without sin cast the first stone." I believe that he who Hates is an assassin; that he who Covets is a thief; that he who Lusts is an adulterer; that the gist of a crime is in its desire. Seeing this—looking into our own hearts— how can we condemn? I believe that Evil is but Ignorance. I believe that "to know all is to forgive all." I believe that there is good in every man; let us help him to manifest it. I believe in the absolute equality of the Man and the Woman—sometimes I think that the odds are slightly in favor of the Woman. I believe in the sacredness of Sex—but I also believe that Sex manifests on the Spiritual and Mental planes as well as on the Physical. And I believe that to the pure all things are pure. I believe that man is immortal— that the Real Self is Spirit, which uses mind and body as its tools, and manifests itself according to the fitness of the tools. I believe that Man is rapidly growing into a new plane of consciousness, in which he will know himself as he is—will recognize the I AM—the Something Within. I believe that there is an Infinite Power in, and of, all things. I believe that, although today we have but the faintest idea of that Power, still we will steadily grow to comprehend it more fully—will get in closer touch with it. Even now we have momentary glimpses of its existence—a momentary consciousness of Oneness with the Absolute. I believe that the greatest happiness consists in maintaining toward the Absolute the attitude of the trusting child, who, feeling no doubt of the parent's love—no doubt of his wisdom— places his little hand in that of the parent, and says "Lead Thou me on." I believe that he who feels towards the Absolute, the trustfulness of the babe which places its little tired head close to the breast of the mother, will also be conscious of the tender answering pressure, as the babe is drawn just a little closer to the mother-heart.*

William Walker Atkinson. THOUGHT VIBRATION OR THE LAW OF ATTRACTION IN THE THOUGHT WORLD.

CHAPTER I.

The Law Of Attraction In The Thought World.

The Universe is governed by Law— one great Law. Its manifestations are multiform, but viewed from the Ultimate there is but *one* Law. We are familiar with some of its manifestations, but are almost totally ignorant of certain others. Still we are learning a little more every day— the veil is being gradually lifted.

We speak learnedly of the Law of Gravitation, but ignore that equally wonderful manifestation, The Law Of Attraction In The Thought World. We are familiar with that wonderful manifestation of Law which draws and holds together the atoms of which matter is composed —we recognize the power of the law that attracts bodies to the earth, that holds the circling worlds 1 in their places, but we close our eyes to *the mighty law that draws to us the things we desire or fear, that makes or mars our lives.*

When we come to see that Thought is a force —a manifestation of energy— having a magnetlike power of attraction, we will begin to understand the why and wherefore of many things that have heretofore seemed dark to us. There is no study that will so well repay the student for his time and trouble as the study of the workings of this mighty law of the world of Thought —the Law of Attraction.

When we think we send out vibrations of a fine ethereal substance, which are as real as the vibrations manifesting light, heat, electricity, magnetism. That these vibrations are not evident to our five senses is no proof that they do not exist. A powerful magnet will send out vibrations and exert a force sufficient to attract to itself a piece of steel weighing a hundred pounds, but we can neither see, taste, smell, hear nor feel the mighty force. These thought vibrations, likewise, cannot be seen, tasted, smelled, heard nor felt in the ordinary way; although it is true there are on record cases of persons peculiarly sensitive to psychic impressions who have perceived powerful thought-waves, and very many of us can testify that we have distinctly *felt* the thought vibrations of others, both whilst in the presence of the sender and at a distance. Telepathy and its kindred phenomena are not idle dreams.

Light and heat are manifested by vibrations of a far lower intensity than those of Thought, but the difference is solely in the rate of vibration. The annals of science throw an interesting light upon this question. Prof. Elisha Gray, an eminent scientist, says in his little book, "The Miracles of Nature":

"There is much food for speculation In the thought that there exist soundwaves that no human ear can hear, and color-waves of light that no eye can see. The long, dark, soundless space between 40,000 and 400,000,000,000,000 vibrations per second, and the infinity of range beyond 700,000,000,000,000 vibrations per second, where light ceases, in the universe of motion, makes it possible to indulge in speculation."

M. M. Williams, in his work entitled "Short Chapters in Science," says:

"There is no gradation between the most rapid undulations or tremblings that produce our sensation of sound, and the slowest of those which give rise to our sensations of gentlest warmth. There is a huge gap between them, wide enough to include another world of motion, all lying between our world of sound and our world of heat and light;

and there is no good reason whatever for supposing that matter is incapable of such intermediate activity, or that such activity may not give rise to intermediate sensations, provided there are organs for taking up and sensifying their movements."

I cite the above authorities merely to give you food for thought, not to attempt to demonstrate to you the fact that thought vibrations exist. The last-named fact has been fully established to the satisfaction of numerous investigators of the subject, and a little reflection will show you that it coincides with your own experiences.

We often hear repeated the well-known Mental Science statement, "Thoughts are Things," and we say these words over without consciously realizing just what is the meaning of the statement. If we fully comprehended the truth of the statement and the natural consequences of the truth back of it, we should understand many things which have appeared dark to us, and would be able to use the wonderful power, Thought Force, just as we use any other manifestation of Energy. As I have said, when we think we set into motion vibrations of a very high degree, *"but just as real as the vibrations of light, heat, sound, electricity."* And when we understand the laws governing the production and transmission of these vibrations we will be able to use them in our daily life, just as we do the better known forms of energy. That we cannot see, hear, weigh or measure these vibrations is no proof that they do not exist. There exist waves of sound which no human ear can hear, although some of these are undoubtedly registered by the ear of some of the insects, and others are caught by delicate scientific instruments invented by man; yet there is a great gap between the sounds registered by the most delicate instrument and the limit which man's mind, reasoning by analogy, knows to be the boundary line between soundwaves and some other forms of vibration. And there are light waves which the eye of man does not register, some of which may be detected by more delicate instruments, and many more so fine

that the instrument has not yet been invented which will detect them, although improvements are being made every year and the unexplored field gradually lessened.

As new instruments are invented, new vibrations are registered by them— *and yet the vibrations were just as real before the invention of the instrument as afterward.* Supposing that we had no instruments to register magnetism—one might be justified in denying the existence of that mighty force, because it could not be tasted, felt, smelt, heard, seen, weighed or measured. And yet the mighty magnet would still send out waves of force sufficient to draw to it pieces of steel weighing hundreds of pounds.

Each form of vibration requires its own form of instrument for registration. At present the human brain seems to be the only instrument capable of registering thought waves, although occultists say that in this century scientists will invent apparatus sufficiently delicate to catch and register such impressions. And from present indications it looks as if the invention named might be expected at any time. The demand exists and undoubtedly will be soon supplied. But to those who have experimented along the lines of practical telepathy no further proof is required than the results of their own experiments.

We are sending out thoughts of greater or less intensity all the time, and we are reaping the results of such thoughts. Not only do our thoughtwaves influence ourselves and others, but they have a drawing power—they attract to us the thoughts of others, things, circumstances, people, "luck," in accord with the character of the thought uppermost in our minds. Thoughts of Love will attract to us the Love of others; circumstances and surroundings in accord with the thought; people who are of like thought. Thoughts of Anger, Hate, Envy, Malice and Jealousy will draw to us the foul brood of kindred thoughts emanating from the minds of others; circumstances in which we will be called upon to manifest these vile thoughts and will receive them in turn from others;

people who will manifest inharmony; and so on. A strong thought, or a thought long continued, will make us the center of attraction for the corresponding thought-waves of others. Like attracts like in the Thought World—as ye sow so shall ye reap. Birds of a feather flock together in the Thought World—curses like chickens come home to roost, and bring their friends with them.

The man or woman who is filled with Love sees Love on all sides and attracts the Love of others. The man with Hate in his heart gets all the Hate he can stand. The man who thinks Fight generally runs up against all the Fight he wants before he gets through. And so it goes, each gets what he calls for over the wireless telegraphy of the Mind. The man who rises in the morning feeling "grumpy" usually manages to have the whole family in the same mood before the breakfast is over. The "nagging" woman generally finds enough to gratify her "nagging" propensity during the day.

This matter of Thought Attraction is a serious one. When you stop to think of it you will see that a man really makes his own surroundings, although he blames others for it. I have known people who understood this law to hold a positive, calm thought and be absolutely unaffected by the inharmony surrounding them. They were like the vessel from which the oil had been poured on the troubled waters—they rested safely and calmly whilst the tempest raged around them. One is not at the mercy of the fitful storms of Thought after he has learned the workings of the Law.

We have passed through the age of physical force on to the age of intellectual supremacy, and are now entering a new and almost unknown field, that of psychic power. This field of energy has its established laws, as well as have the others, and we should acquaint ourselves with them or we will be crowded to the wall as are the ignorant on the planes of effort. I will endeavor to make plain to you the great underlying principles of this new field of energy which is opening up before us, that you may be able to make use of this great power and apply it for legitimate and worthy purposes, just as men are using steam, electricity and other forms of energy today.

CHAPTER II

Thought-waves And Their Process Of Reproduction

Like a stone thrown into the water, thought produces ripples and waves which spread out over the great ocean of thought. There is this difference, however: the waves on the water move only on a level plane in all directions, whereas thought-waves move in all directions from a common center, just as do the rays from the sun.

Just as we here on earth are surrounded by a great sea of air, so are we surrounded by a great sea of Mind. Our thought-waves move through this vast mental ether, extending, however, in all directions, as I have explained, becoming somewhat lessened in intensity according to the distance traversed, because of the friction occasioned by the waves coming in contact with the great body of Mind surrounding us on all sides.

These thought-waves have other qualities differing from the waves on the water. *They have the property of reproducing themselves.* In this respect they resemble sound-waves rather than waves upon the water. Just as a note of the violin will cause the thin glass to vibrate and "sing," so will a strong thought tend to awaken similar vibrations in minds attuned to receive it. Many of the "stray thoughts" which come to us are but reflections or answering vibrations to some strong thought sent out by another. But unless our minds are attuned to receive it, the thought will not likely affect us. If we are thinking high and great thoughts, our minds acquire a certain keynote corresponding to the character of the thoughts we have been thinking. And, this keynote once established, we will be apt to catch the vibrations of other minds keyed to the same thought. On the other hand, let us get into the habit of thinking thoughts of an opposite character, and we will soon be echoing the low order of thought emanating from the minds of the thousands thinking along the same lines.

We are largely what we have thought ourselves into being, the balance being represented by the character of the suggestions and thought of others, which have reached us either directly by verbal suggestions or telepathically by meansof such thought-waves. Our general mental attitude, however, determines the character of the thought-waves received from others as well as the thoughts emanating from ourselves. We receive only such thoughts as are in harmony with the general mental attitude held by ourselves; the thoughts not in harmony affecting us very little, as they awaken no response in us.

The man who believes thoroughly in himself and maintains a positive strong mental attitude of Confidence and Determination is not likely to be affected by the adverse and negative thoughts of Discouragement and Failure emanating from the minds of other persons in whom these last qualities predominate. At the same time these negative thoughts, if they reach one whose mental attitude is pitched on a low key, deepen his negative state and add fuel to the fire which is consuming his strength, or, if you prefer this figure, serve to further smother the fire of his energy and activity.

We attract to us the thoughts of others of the same order of thought. The man who thinks success will be apt to get into tune with the minds of others thinking likewise, and they will help him, and he them. The man who allows his mind to dwell constantly upon thoughts of failure brings himself into close touch with the minds of other "failure" people, and each will tend to pull the other down still more. The man who thinks that all is evil is apt to see much evil, and will be brought into contact with others who will seem to prove his theory. And the man who looks for good in everything and everybody will be likely to attract to himself the things and people corresponding to his thought. We generally see that for which we look.

You will be able to carry this idea

more clearly if you will think of the Marconi wireless instruments, which receive the vibrations only from the sending instrument which has been attuned to the same key, while other telegrams are passing through the air in near vicinity without affecting the instrument. The same law applies to the operations of thought. We receive only that which corresponds to our mental attunement. If we have been discouraged, we may rest assured that we have dropped into a negative key, and have been affected not only by our own thoughts but have also received the added depressing thoughts of similar character which are constantly being sent out from the minds of other unfortunates who have not yet learned the law of attraction in the thought world. And if we occasionally rise to heights of enthusiasm and energy, how quickly we feel the inflow of the courageous, daring, energetic, positive thoughts being sent out by the live men and women of the world. We recognize this without much trouble when we come in personal contact with people and feel their vibrations, depressing or invigorating, as the case may be. But the same law operates when we are not in their presence, although less strongly.

The mind has many degrees of pitch, ranging from the highest positive note to the lowest negative note, with many notes in between, varying in pitch according to their respective distance from the positive or negative extreme.

When your mind is operating along positive lines you feel strong, buoyant, bright, cheerful, happy, confident and courageous, and are enabled to do your work well, to carry out your intentions, and progress on your road to Success. You send out strong positive thought, which affects others and causes them to co-operate with you or to follow your lead, according to their own mental keynote.

When you are playing on the extreme negative end of the mental keyboard you feel depressed, weak, passive, dull, fearful, cowardly. And you find yourself unable to make progress or to succeed. And your effect upon others is practically *nil*. You are led by, rather than leading others, and are used as a human door-mat or football by more positive persons.

In some persons the positive element seems to predominate, and in others the negative quality seems to be more in evidence. There are, of course, widely varying degrees of positiveness and negativeness, and B may be negative to A, while positive to C. When two people first meet there is generally a silent mental conflict in which their respective minds test their quality of positiveness, and fix their relative position toward each other. This process may be unconscious in many cases, but it occurs nevertheless. The adjustment is often automatic, but occasionally the struggle is so sharp—the opponents being so well matched—that the matter forces itself into the consciousness of the two people. Sometimes both parties are so much alike in their degrees of positiveness that they practically fail to come to terms, mentally; they never really are able to get along with each other, and they are either mutually repelled and separate or else stay together amid constant broils and wrangling.

We are positive or negative to every one with whom we have relations. We may be positive to our children, our employes and dependents, but we are at the same time negative to others to whom we occupy inferior positions, or whom we have allowed to assert themselves over us.

Of course, something may occur and we will suddenly become more positive than the man or woman to whom we have heretofore been negative. We frequently see cases of this kind. And as the knowledge of these mental laws becomes more general we will see many more instances of persons asserting themselves and making use of their new-found power.

But remember you possess the power to raise the keynote of your mind to a positive pitch by an effort of the will. And, of course, it is equally true that you may allow yourself to drop into a low, negative note by carelessness or a weak will.

There are more people on the negative plane of thought than on the positive plane, and consequently there are more negative thought vibrations in operation in our mental atmosphere. But, happily for us, this is counterbalanced by the fact that a positive thought is infinitely more powerful than a negative one, and if by force of will we raise ourselves to a higher mental key we can shut out the depressing thoughts and may take up the vibrations corresponding with our changed mental attitude. This is one of the secrets of the affirmations and auto-suggestions used by the several schools of Mental Science and other New Thought cults. There is no particular merit in affirmations of themselves, but they serve a twofold purpose: (1) They tend to establish new mental attitudes within us and act wonderfully in the direction of character building—the science of making ourselves over. (2) They tend to raise the mental keynote so that we may get the benefit of the positive thought-waves of others on the same plane of thought.

Whether or not we believe in them, we are constantly making affirmations. The man who asserts that he can and will do a thing—and asserts it earnestly—develops in himself the qualities conducive to the well doing of that thing, and at the same time places his mind in the propef key to receive all the thought-waves likely to help him in the doing. If, on the other hand, one says and feels that he is going to fail, he will choke and smother the thoughts coming from his own subconscious mentality which are intended to help him, and at the same time will place himself in tune with the Failure-thought of the world— and there is plenty of the latter kind of thought around, I can tell you.

Do not allow yourselves to be effected by the adverse and negative thoughts of those around you. Rise to the upper chambers of your mental dwelling, and key yourself up to a strong pitch, away above the vibrations on the lower planes of thought. Then you will not only be immune to their negative vibrations but will be in touch with the great body of strong positive thought coming from those of your own plane of development.

My aim will be to direct and train you in the proper use of thought and will, that you may have yourself well in hand and may be able to strike the positive key at any moment you may feel it necessary. It is not necessary to strike the extreme note on all occasions. The better plan is to keep yourself in a comfortable key, without much strain, and to have the means at command whereby you can raise the pitch at once when occasion demands. By this knowledge you will not be at the mercy of the old automatic action of the mind, but may have it well under your own control.

Development of the will is very much like the development of a muscle—a matter of practice and gradual improvement. At first it is apt to be tiresome, but at each trial one grows stronger until the new strength becomes real and permanent. Many of us have made ourselves positive under sudden calls or emergencies. We are in the habit of "bracing up" when occasion demands. But by intelligent practice you will be so much strengthened that your habitual state will be equal to your "bracing up" stage now, and then when you find it necessary to apply the spur you will be able to reach a stage not dreamed of at present.

Do not understand me as advocating a high tension continuously. This is not at all desirable, not only because it is apt to be too much of a strain upon you but also because you will find it desirable to relieve the tension at times and become receptive that you may absorb impressions. It is well to be able to relax and assume a certain degree of receptiveness, knowing that you are always able to spring back to the more positive state at will. The habitually strongly positive man loses much enjoyment and recreation. Positive, you give out expressions; receptive, you take in impressions. Positive, you are a teacher; receptive, a pupil. It is not only a good thing to be a good teacher, but it is also very important to be a good listener at times.

CHAPTER III

A Talk About The Mind

Man has but one mind, but he has many mental faculties, each faculty being capable of functioning along two different lines of mental effort. There are no distinct dividing lines separating the two several functions of a faculty, but they shade into each other as do the colors of the spectrum.

An Active effort of any faculty of the mind is the result of a direct impulse imparted at the time of the effort. A Passive effort of any faculty of the mind is the result of either a preceding Active effort of the same mind; an Active effort of another along the lines of suggestion; Thought Vibrations from the mind of another; Thought impulses from an ancestor, transmitted by the laws of heredity (including impulses transmitted from generation to generation from the time of the original vibratory impulse imparted by the Primal Cause—which impulses gradually unfold, and unsheath, when the proper state of evolutionary development is reached).

The Active effort is new-born—fresh from the mint, whilst the Passive effort is of less recent creation, and, in fact, is often the result of vibratory impulses imparted in ages long past. The Active effort makes its own way, brushing aside the impeding vines and kicking from its path the obstructing stones. The Passive effort travels along the beaten path.

A thought-impulse, or motion-impulse, originally caused by an Active effort of faculty, may become by continued repetition, or habit, strictly automatic, the impulse given it by the repeated Active effort developing a strong momentum, which carries it on, along Passive lines, until stopped by another Active effort or its direction changed by the same cause.

On the other hand, thought-impulses, or motion-impulses, continued along Passive lines may be terminated or corrected by an Active effort. The Active function creates, changes or destroys. The Passive function carries on the work given it by the Active function and obeys orders and suggestions.

The Active function produces the

thoughthabit, or motion-habit, and imparts to it the vibrations which carry it on along the Passive lines thereafter. The Active function also has the power to send forth vibrations which neutralize the momentum of the thought-habit, or motionhabit; it also is able to launch a *new* thoughthabit, or motion-habit, with stronger vibrations, which overcomes and absorbs the first thought, or motion, and substitutes the new one.

All thought-impulses, or motion-impulses, once started on their errands, continue to vibrate along passive lines until corrected or terminated by subsequent impulses imparted by the Active function, or other controlling power. The continuance of the original impulse adds momentum and force to it, and renders its correction or termination more difficult. This explains that which is called "the force of habit." I think that this will be readily understood by those who have struggled to overcome a habit which had been easily acquired. The Law applies to good habits as well as bad. The moral is obvious.

Several of the faculties of the mind often combine to produce a single manifestation. A task to be performed may call for the combined exercise of several faculties, some of which may manifest by Active effort and others by Passive effort.

The meeting of new conditions—new problems —calls for the exercise of Active effort; whilst a familiar problem, or task, can be easily handled by the Passive effort without the assistance of his more enterprising brother.

There is in Nature an instinctive tendency of living organisms to perform certain actions, the tendency of an organized body to seek that which satisfies the wants of its organism. This tendency is sometimes called Appetency. It is really a Passive mental impulse, originating with the impetus imparted by the Primal Cause, and transmitted along the lines of evolutionary development, gaining strength and power as it progresses. The impulse of the Primal Cause is assisted by the powerful upward attraction exerted by The Absolute.

In plant life this tendency is plainly discernible, ranging from the lesser exhibitions in the lower types to the greater in the higher types. It is that which is generally spoken of as the "life force" in plants. It is, however, a manifestation of rudimentary mentation, functioning along the lines of Passive effort. In some of the higher forms of plant life there appears a faint color of independent "life action"—a faint indication of choice of volition. Writers on plant life relate many remarkable instances of this phenomenon. It is, undoubtedly, an exhibition of rudimentary Active mentation.

In the lower animal kingdom a very high degree of Passive mental effort is found. And, varying in degree in the several families and species, a considerable amount of Active mentation is apparent. The lower animal undoubtedly possesses Reason only in a lesser degree than man, and, in fact, the display of volitional mentation exhibited by an intelligent animal is often nearly as high as that shown by the lower types of man or by a young child.

As a child, before birth, shows in its body the stages of the physical evolution of man, so does a child, before and after birth—until maturity— manifest the stages of the *mental* evolution of man.

Man, the highest type of life yet produced, at least upon this planet, shows the highest form of Passive mentation, and also a much higher development of Active mentation than is seen in the lower animals, and yet the degrees of that power vary widely among the different races of men. Evai among men of our race the different degrees of Active mentation are plainly noticeable; these degrees not depending by any means upon the amount of "culture," social position or educational advantages possessed by the individual. Mental Culture and Mental Development are two very different things.

You have but to look around you to see the different stages of the development of Active mentation in man. The reasoning of many men is scarcely more than Passive mentation, exhibiting but little of the qualities of volitional thought. They prefer to let other men think for them. Active mentation tires them and they find the instinctive, automatic, Passive mental process much easier. Their minds work along the lines of least resistance. They are but little more than human sheep.

Among the lower animals and the lower types of men Active mentation is largely confined to the grosser faculties—the more material plane; the higher mental faculties working along the instinctive, automatic lines of the Passive function.

As the lower forms of life progressed in the evolutionary scale, they developed new faculties, which were latent within them. These faculties always manifested in the form of rudimentary Passive functioning, and afterwards worked up, through higher Passive forms, until the Active functions were brought into play. The evolutionary process still continues, the invariable tendency being toward the goal of highly developed Active mentation. This evolutionary progress is caused by the vibratory impulse imparted by the Primal Cause, aided by the uplifting attraction of The Absolute.

This law of evolution is still in progress, and man is beginning to develop new powers of mind, which, of course, are first manifesting themselves along the lines of Passive effort. Some men have developed these new faculties to a considerable degree, and it is possible that before long Man will be able to exercise them along the line of their Active functions. In fact, this power has already been attained by a few. This is the secret of the Oriental occultists, and of some of their Occidental brethren.

The amenability of the mind to the Will can be increased by properly directed practice. That which we are in the habit of referring to as the "strengthening of the Will" is in reality the training of the mind to recognize and absorb the Power Within. The Will is strong enough; it does not need strengthening, but the mind needs to be trained to receive and act upon the suggestions of the Will. The Will is the outward manifestation of the I AM. The Will current is flowing in full strength along the spiritual wires; but you must learn how to raise the trolley-pole to touch it before the mental car will move. This is a somewhat different idea from that which you have been in the habit of receiving from writers on the subject of Will Power, but it is correct, as you will demonstrate to your own satisfaction if you will follow up the subject by experiments along the proper lines.

The attraction of The Absolute is drawing man upward, and the vibratory force of the Primal Impulse has not yet exhausted itself. The time of evolutionary development has come when man can help himself. The man who understands the Law can accomplish wonders by means of the development of the powers of the mind; whilst the man who turns his back upon the truth will suffer from his lack of knowledge of the Law.

He who understands the laws of his mental being, develops his latent powers and uses them intelligently. He does not despise his Passive mental functions, but makes good use of them also, charges them with the duties for which they are best fitted, and is able to obtain wonderful results from their work, having mastered them and trained them to do the bidding of the Higher Self. When they fail to do their work properly he regulates them, and his knowledge prevents him from meddling with them unintelligently, and thereby doing himself harm. He develops the faculties and powers latent within him and learns how to manifest them along the line of Active mentation as well as Passive. He knows that the *real* man within him is the master to whom both Active and Passive functions are but tools. He has banished Fear, and enjoys Freedom. He has found *himself.* He Has Learned THE SECRET OF THE I AM.

CHAPTER TV

Mind Building

Man can build up his mind and make it what he wills. In fact, we are mind-building every hour of our lives, either consciously or unconsciously. The majority of us are doing the work unconsciously, but those who have seen a little below the surface of things have taken the matter in hand and have become conscious creators of their own mentality. They are no longer subject to the suggestions and influences of others but have become masters of themselves. They assert the "I," and compel obedience from the subordinate mental faculties. The "I" is the sovereign of the mind, and what we call WILL is the instrument of the "I." Of course, there is something back of this, and the Universal Will is higher than the Will of the Individual, but the latter is in much closer touch with the Universal Will than is generally supposed, and when one conquers the lower self, and asserts the "I," he so becomes in close touch with the Universal Will and partakes largely of its wonderful power. The moment one asserts the "I," and "finds himself," he establishes a close connection between the Individual Will and the Universal Will. But before he is able to avail himself of the mighty power at his command, he must first effect the Mastery of the lower self.

Think of the absurdity of Man claiming to manifest powers, when he is the slave of the lower parts of his mental being, which should be subordinate. Think of a man being the slave of his moods, passions, animal appetites and lower faculties, and at the same time trying to claim the benefits of the Will. Now, I am not preaching asceticism, which seems to me to be a confession of weakness. I am speaking of Self-Mastery— the assertion of the *"I"* over the subordinate parts of oneself. In the higher view of the subject, this "I" is the only *real* Self, and the rest is the non-self; but our space does not permit the discussion of this point, and we will use the word "self" as meaning the entire man. Before a man can assert the "I" in its full strength he must obtain the complete mastery of the subordinate parts of the self. All things are good when we learn to master them, but no thing is good when it masters us. Just so long as we allow the lower portions of the self to give us orders, we are slaves. It is only when the "I" mounts his throne and lifts the sceptre, that order is established

and things assume their proper relation to each other.

We are finding no fault with those who are swayed by their lower selves— they are in a lower grade of evolution, and will work up in time. But we are calling the attention of those who are ready, to the fact that the Sovereign must assert his will, and that the subjects must obey. Orders must be given and carried out. Rebellion must be put down, and the rightful authority insisted upon. And the time to do it is Now.

You have been allowing your rebellious subjects to keep the King from his throne. You have been allowing the mental kingdom to be misgoverned by irresponsible faculties. You have been the slaves of Appetite, Unworthy Thoughts, Passion and Negativeness. The Will has been set aside and Low Desire has usurped the throne. It is time to re-establish order in the mental kingdom.

You are able to assert the mastery over any emotion, appetite, passion or class of thoughts by the assertion of the Will. You can order Fear to go to the rear; Jealousy to leave your presence; Hate to depart from your sight; Anger to hide itself; Worry to cease troubling you; Uncontrolled Appetite and Passion to bow in submission and to become humble slaves instead of masters—all by the assertion of the "I." You may surround yourself with the glorious company of Courage, Love and Self-Control, by the same means. You may put down the rebellion and secure peace and order in your mental kingdom if you will but utter the mandate and insist upon its execution. Before you march forth to empire, you must establish the proper internal conditions —must show your ability to govern your own kingdom. The first battle is the conquest of the lesser self by the Real Self.

Affirmation. / *Am Asserting the Mastery of My Real Self.* Repeat these words *earnestly* and positively during the day, at least once an hour, and particularly when you are confronted with conditions which tempt you to act on the lines of the lesser self instead of following the course dictated by the Real

Self. In the moment of doubt and hesitation, say these words earnestly, and your way will be made clear to you. Repeat them several times after you retire and settle yourself to sleep. But be sure to back up the words with the thought inspiring them, and do not merely repeat them parrot-like. Form the mental image of the Real Self asserting its mastery over the lower planes of your mind—see the King on his Throne. You will become conscious of an influx of new thought, and things which have seemed hard for you will suddenly become much easier. You will feel that you have yourself well in hand, and that YOU are the master and not the slave. The thought you are holding will manifest itself in action, and you will steadily grow to become that which you have in mind.

Exercise.

Fix the mind firmly on the higher Self and draw inspiration from it when you feel led to yield to the promptings of the lower part of your nature. When you are tempted to burst into Anger—assert the "I," and your voice will drop. Anger is unworthy of the developed Self. When you feel vexed and cross, remember what you are, and rise above your feeling. When you feel Fearful, remember that the Real Self fears nothing, and assert Courage. When you feel Jealousy inciting, think of your higher nature, and laugh. And so on, asserting the Real Self and not allowing the things on the lower plane of mentality to disturb you. They are unworthy of you, and must be taught to keep their places. Do not allow these things to master you—they should be your subjects, not your masters. You must get away from this plane, and the only way to do so is to cut loose from these phases of thought which have been "running things" to suit themselves. You may have trouble at the start, but keep at it and you will have that satisfaction which comes only from conquering the lower parts of our nature. You have been a slave long enough—now is the time to free yourselves. If you will follow these exercises faithfully you will be a different being by the end of the year, and will look back with a pitying smile to your former condition. But it takes work. This is not child's play, but a task for earnest men and women. Will You make the effort?

CHAPTER V

The Secret Of The Will

While psychologists may differ in their theories regarding the nature of the Will, none deny its existence, nor question its power. All persons recognize the power of strong Will—all see how it may be used to overcome the greatest obstacles. But few realize that the Will may be developed and strengthened by intelligent practice. They feel that they could accomplish wonders if they had a strong Will, but instead of attempting to develop it, they content themselves with vain regrets. They sigh, but do nothing.

Those who have investigated the subject closely know that Will Power, with all its latent possibilities and mighty powers, may be developed, disciplined, controlled and directed, just as may be any other of Nature's forces. It does not matter what theory you may entertain about the nature of the Will, you will obtain the results if you practice intelligently.

Personally, I have a somewhat odd theory about the Will. I believe that every man has, potentially, a strong Will, and that all he has to do is to train his mind to make use of it. I think that in the higher regions of the mind of every man is a great store of Will Power awaiting his use. The Will current is running along the psychic wires, and all that it is necessary to do is to raise the mental trolley-pole and bring down the power for your use. And the supply is unlimited, for your little storage battery is connected with the great power house of the Universal Will Power, and the power is inexhaustible. Your Will does not need training—but your Mind does. The mind is the instrument and the supply of Will Power is proportionate to the fineness of the instrument through which it manifests. But you needn't accept this theory if you don't like it. This lesson will fit your theory as well as mine.

He who has developed his mind so that it will allow the Will Power to manifest through it, has opened up wonderful possibilities for himself. Not only has he found a great power at his command, but he is able to bring into play, and use, faculties, talents and abilities of whose existence he has not dreamed. This secret of the Will is the magic key which opens all doors.

The late Donald G. Mitchell once wrote: *"Resolve* is what makes a man manifest; not puny resolve, but crude determination; not errant purpose—but that strong and indefatigable will which treads down difficulties and danger, as a boy treads down the heaving frostlands of winter; which kindles his eye and brain with a proud pulse-beat toward the unattainable. Will makes men giants."

Many of us feel that if we would but exert our Will, we might accomplish wonders. But somehow we do not seem to want to take the trouble—at any rate, we do not get to the actual willing point. We put it off from time to time, and talk vaguely of "some day," but that some day never comes.

We instinctively feel the power of the Will, but we haven't enough energy to exercise it, and so drift along with the tide, unless perhaps some friendly difficulty arises, some helpful obstacle appears in our path, or some kindly pain stirs us into action, in either of which cases we are compelled to assert our Will and thus begin to accomplish something.

The trouble with us is that we do not want to do the thing enough to make us exert our Will Power. *We don't want to hard enough.* We are mentally lazy and of weak Desire. If you do not like the word Desire substitute for it the word "Aspiration." (Some people call the lower impulses Desires, and the higher, Aspirations— it's all a matter of words, take your choice.) That is the trouble. Let a man be in danger of losing his life—let a woman be in danger of losing a great love—and you will witness a startling exhibition of Will Power from an unexpected source. Let a woman's child be threatened with danger, and she will manifest a degree of Courage and Will that sweeps all before it. And yet

the same woman will quail before a domineering husband, and will lack the Will to perform a simple task. A boy will do all sorts of work if he but considers it play, and yet he can scarcely force himself to cut a little fire-wood. Strong Will follows strong Desire. If you really want to do a thing very much, you can usually develop the Will Power to accomplish it.

The trouble is that you have not really *wanted* to do these things, and yet you blame your Will. You say that you *do* want to do it, but if you stop to think you will see that you really want to do something else more than the thing in question. You are not willing to pay the price of attainment. Stop a moment and analyze this statement and apply it to your own case.

You are mentally lazy—that's the trouble. Don't talk to me about not having enough Will. You have a great storehouse of Will awaiting your use, but you are too lazy to use it. Now, if you are really in earnest about this matter, get to work and first find out what you really want to do—then start to work and *do* it. Never mind about the Will Power—you'll find a full supply of that whenever you need it. The thing to do is to get to the point where you will *resolve* to Will. That's the real test— *the resolving.* Think of these things a little, and make up your mind whether or not you really want to be a Wilier sufficiently hard to get to work.

Many excellent essays and books have been written on this subject, all of which agree regarding the greatness of Will Power, the most enthusiastic terms being used; but few have anything to say about how this power may be acquired by those who have it not, or who possess it in but a limited degree. Some have given

V exercises designed to "strengthen" the Will, which exercises really strengthen the Mind so that it is able to draw upon its store of power. But they have generally overlooked the fact that in auto-suggestion is to be found the secret of the development of the mind so that it may become the efficient instrument of the Will.

what you say. You must use Faith at the start, and use the words with a *confident expectation* of the result. Hold the steady thought that you *are* drawing on your storehouse of Will Power, and before long you will find that thought is taking form in action, and that your Will Power is manifesting itself. You will feel an influx of strength with each repetition of the words. You will find yourself overcoming difficulties and bad habits, and will be surprised at how things are being smoothed out for you.

Exercise

Perform at least *one* disagreeable task each day during the month. If there is any specially disagreeable task which you would like to shirk, *that* is the one for you to perform. This is not given you in order to make you self-sacrificing or meek, or anything of that sort—it is given you to *exercise your Will.* Anyone can do a pleasant thing cheerfully, but it takes Will to do the unpleasant thing cheerfully; and that is how you must do the work. It will prove a most valuable discipline to you. Try it for a month and you will see where it "comes in." If you shirk this exercise you had better stop right here and acknowledge that you do not want Will Power, and are content to stay where you are and remain a weakling.

CHAPTER VI

How To Become Immune To Injurious Thought Attraction

The first thing to do is to begin to "cut out" Fear and Worry. Fearthought is the cause of much unhappiness and many

You have been told this thing over again, but it will bear re- Fear is a habit of mind which fastened upon us by negative ught, but from which we may selves by individual effort and ance.

g expectancy is a powerful He of the strong, confident de- acts to him the things best cal- to aid him—persons, things, cir- ices, surroundings; if he desires pefully, trustfully, confidently, And, equally true, he who Fears generally manages to start into n forces which will cause the uning he feared to come upon him. Don't you see, the man who Fears really *expects* the feared thing, and in the eyes of the Law it is the same as if he really had wished for or desired it? The Law is operative in both cases—the principle is the same.

The best way to overcome the habit of Fear is to assume the mental attitude of Courage, just as the best way to get rid of darkness is to let in the light. It is a waste of time to fight a negative thought-habit by recognizing its force and trying to *deny* it out of existence by mighty efforts. The best, surest, easiest and quickest method is to assume the existence of the positive thought desired in its place; and by constantly dwelling upon the positive thought, manifest it into objective reality.

Therefore, instead of repeating, "I'm not afraid," say boldly, "I am full of Courage," "I am Courageous." You must assert, "There's nothing to fear," which, although in the nature of a denial, simply denies the reality of the object causing fear rather than admitting the fear itself and then denying it.

To overcome Fear, one should hold firmly to the mental attitude of Courage. He should think Courage, say Courage, act Courage. He should keep the mental picture of Courage before him all the time, until it becomes his normal mental attitude. Hold the ideal firmly before you and you will gradually grow to its attainment—the ideal will become manifest.

Let the word "Courage" sink deeply into your mind, and then hold it firmly there until the mind fastens it in place. Think of yourself as being Courageous—see yourself as acting with Courage in trying situations. Realize that there is nothing to Fear—that Worry and Fear never helped anyone, and never will. Realize that Fear paralyzes effort, and that Courage promotes activity.

The confident, fearless, expectant, "I Can and I Will" man is a mighty magnet. He attracts to himself just what is needed for his success. Things seem to come his way, and people say he is "lucky." Nonsense! "Luck" has nothing to do with it. It's all in the Mental Attitude. And the Mental Attitude of the "I Can't" or the "I'm Afraid" man also determines his measure of success. There's no mystery whatsoever about it. You have but to look about you to realize the truth of what I have said. Did you ever know a successful man who did not have the "I Can and I Will" thought strong within him? Why, he will walk all around the "I Can't" man, who has perhaps even more ability. The first mental attitude brought to the surface latent qualities, as well as attracted help from outside; whilst the second mental attitude not only attracted I Can't" people and things, but also kept the man's own powers from manifesting themselves. I have demonstrated the correctness of these views, and so have many others, and the number of people who *know* these things is growing every day.

Don't waste your Thought-Force, but use it to advantage. Stop attracting to yourself failure, unhappiness, inharmony, sorrow—begin now and send out a current of bright, positive, happy thought. Let your prevailing thought be "I Can and I Will;" *think "I* Can and I Will;" *dream "I* Can and I Will;" *say "I* Can and I Will;" *act "I* Can and I Will." Live on the "I Can and I Will" plane, and before you are aware of it, you will feel the new vibrations manifesting themselves in action; will see them bring results; will be conscious of the new point of view; will realize that your own is coming to you. You will feel better, act better, see better, BE better in every way, after you join the "I Can and I Will" brigade.

Fear is the parent of Worry, Hate, Jealousy, Malice, Anger, Discontent, Failure and all the rest. The man who rids himself of Fear will find that the rest of the brood have disappeared. The only way to be Free is to get rid of Fear. Tear it out by the roots. I regard the conquest of Fear as the first important step to be taken by those who wish to master the application of Thought Force. So long as Fear masters you, you are in no condition to make progress in the realm of Thought, and I must insist that you start to work at once to get rid of this obstruction. You CAN do it—if you only go about it in earnest. And when you have ridded yourself of the vile thing, life will seem entirely different to you—you will feel happier, freer, stronger, more positive, and will be more successful in every undertaking of Life.

Start in today, make up your mind that this intruder must GO—do not compromise matters with him, but insist upon an absolute surrender on his part. You will find the task difficult at first, but each time you oppose him he will grow weaker, and you will be stronger. Shut off his nourishment—starve him to death—he cannot live in a thought-atmosphere of Fearlessness. So, start to fill your mind with good, strong, Fearless thoughts—keep yourself busy thinking Fearlessness, and Fear will die of his own accord. Fearlessness is positive—Fear is negative, and you may be sure that the positive will prevail.

So long as Fear is around with his "but," "if," "suppose," "I'm afraid," "I can't," "what if," and all the rest of his cowardly suggestions, you will not be able to use your Thought Force to the best advantage. Once get him out of the way, you will have clear sailing, and every inch of thought-sail will catch the wind. He is a Jonah. Overboard with him! (The whale who swallows him will have my sympathy.)

I advise that you start in to do some of the things which you feel you could do if you were not *afraid* to try. Start to work to do these things, affirming "Courage" all the way through, and you will be surprised to see how the changed mental attitude will clear away obstacles from your path, and will make things very much easier than you had anticipated. Exercises of this kind will develop you wonderfully, and you will be much gratified at the result of a little practice along these lines.

There are many things before you awaiting accomplishment, which you can master if you will only throw aside the yoke of Fear—if you will only refuse to accept the race suggestion, and will boldly assert the "I" and its power. And the best way to vanquish Fear is to assert "Courage" and stop thinking of Fear. By this plan you will train the mind into new habits of thought, thus eradicating the old negative thoughts which have been pulling you down, and holding you back. Take the word "Courage" with you as your watchword and manifest it in action.

Remember, the only thing to fear is Fear, and —well, don't even *fear* Fear, for he's a cowardly chap at the best, who will run if you show a brave front.

CHAPTER VII The Transmutation Of Negative Thought

Worry is the child of Fear—if you kill out Fear, Worry will die for want of nourishment. This advice is very old, and yet it is always worthy of repetition, for it is a lesson of which we are greatly in need. Some people think that if we kill out Fear and Worry we will never be able to accomplish anything. I have read editorials in the great journals in which the writers held that without Worry one can never accomplish any of the great tasks of life, because Worry is necessary to stimulate interest and work. This is nonsense, no matter who utters it. Worry never helped one to accomplish anything; on the contrary, it stands in the way of accomplishment and attainment.

The motive underlying action and "doing things" is Desire and Interest. If one earnestly desires a thing, he naturally becomes very much interested in its accomplishment, and is quick to so seize upon anything likely to help him to gain the thing he wants. More than that, his mind starts up a work on the sub-conscious plane that brings into the field of consciousness many ideas of value and importance. Desire and Interest are the causes that result in success. Worry is not Desire. It is true that if one's surroundings and environments become intolerable, he is driven in desperation to some efforts that will result in throwing off the undesirable conditions and in the acquiring of those more in harmony with his desire. But this is only another form of Desire—the man desires something different from what he has; and when his desire becomes strong enough his entire interest is given to the task, he makes a mighty effort, and the change is accomplished. But it wasn't Worry that caused the effort. Worry could content itself with wringing its hands and moaning "Woe is me," and wearing its nerves to a frazzle, and accomplishing nothing. Desire acts differently. It grows stronger as the man's conditions become intolerable, and finally when he feels the hurt so strongly that he can't stand it any longer, he says, "I *won't* stand this any longer—I *will* make a change," and lo! then Desire springs into action. The man keeps on "wanting" a change the worst way (which is the *best* way) and his Interest and Attention being given to the task of deliverance, he begins to make things move. Worry never accomplished anything. Worry is negative and death producing. Desire and Ambition are positive and life producing. A man may worry himself to death and yet nothing will be accomplished, but let that man transmute his worry and discontent into Desire and Interest, coupled with a belief that he is able to make the change—the "I Can and I Will" idea—then something happens.

Yes, Fear and Worry must go before we can do much. One must proceed to cast out these negative intruders, and replace them with Confidence and Hope. Transmute Worry into keen Desire. Then you will find that Interest is awakened, and you will begin to think things of interest to you. Thoughts will come to you from the great reserve stock in your mind and you will start to manifest them in action. Moreover you will be placing yourself in harmony with similar thoughts of others, and will draw to you aid and assistance from the great volume of thought waves with which the world is filled. One draws to himself thought waves corresponding in character with the nature of the prevailing thoughts in his own mind—his mental attitude. Then again he begins to set into motion the great Law of Attraction, whereby he draws to him others likely to help him, and is, in turn, attracted to others who can aid him. This Law of Attraction is no joke, no metaphysical absurdity, but is a great live working principle of Nature, as anyone may learn by experimenting and observing.

To succeed in anything you must want it very much—Desire must be in evidence in order to attract. The man of weak desires attracts very little to himself. The stronger the Desire the greater the force set into motion. You must want a thing hard enough before you can get it. You must want it more than you do the things around you, and you must be prepared to pay the price for it. The price is the throwing overboard of certain lesser desires that stand in the way of the accomplishment of the greater one. Comfort, ease, leisure, amusements, and many other things may have to go (not always, though). It all depends on what you want. As a rule, the greater the thing desired, the greater the price to be paid for it. Nature believes in adequate compensation. But if you really Desire a thing in earnest, you will pay the price without question; for the Desire will dwarf the importance of the other things.

You say that you want a thing very much, and are doing everything possible toward its attainment? Pshaw! you are only playing Desire. Do you want the thing as much as a prisoner wants freedom—as much as a dying man wants life? Look at the almost miraculous things accomplished by prisoners desiring freedom. Look how they work through steel plates and stone walls with a bit of stone. Is your desire as strong as that? Do you work for the desired thing as if your life depended upon it?

Nonsense! you don't know what Desire is. I tell you if a man wants a thing as much as the prisoner wants freedom, or as much as a strongly vital man wants life, then that man will be able to sweep away obstacles and impediments apparently immovable. The key to attainment is Desire, Confidence, and Will. This key will open many doors.

Fear paralyzes Desire—it scares the life out of it. You must get rid of Fear. There have been times in my life when Fear would get hold of me and take a good, firm grip on my vitals, and I would lose all hope; all interest; all ambition; all desire. But, thank the Lord, I have always managed to throw off the grip of the monster and face my difficulty like a man; and lo! things would seem to be straightened out for me somehow. Either the difficulty would melt away, or I would be given means to overcome it, or get around, or under or over it. It is strange how this works. No matter how great is the difficulty, when we finally face it with courage and confidence in ourselves, we seem to pull through somehow, and then we begin to wonder what we were scared about. This is not a mere fancy, it is the working of a mighty law, which we do not as yet fully understand, but which we may prove at any time.

People often ask: "It's all very well for you New Thought people to say 'Don't worry,' but what's a person to do when he thinks of all the possible things ahead of him, which might upset him and his plans?" Well, all that I can say is that the man is foolish to bother about thinking of troubles to come at some time in the future. The majority of things that we worry about don't come to pass at all; a large proportion of the others come in a milder form than we had anticipated, and there are always other things which come at the same time which help us to overcome the trouble. The future holds in store for us not only difficulties to be overcome, but also agents to help us in overcoming the difficulties. Things adjust themselves. We are prepared for any trouble which may come upon us, and when the time comes we somehow find ourselves able

to meet it. God not only tempers the wind to the shorn lamb, but He also tempers the shorn lamb to the wind. The wind and the shearing do not come together; there is usually enough time for the lamb to get seasoned, and then he generally grows new wool before the cold blast comes.

It has been well said that nine-tenths of the worries are over things which never come to pass, and that the other tenth is over things of little or no account. So what's the use in using up all your reserve force in fretting over future troubles, if this be so? Better wait until your troubles really come before you worry. You will find that by this storing up of energy you will be able to meet about any sort of trouble that comes your way.

What is it that uses up all the energy in the average man or woman, anyway? Is it the real overcoming of difficulties, or the worrying about impending troubles? It's always "Tomorrow, tomorrow," and yet tomorrow never comes just as we feared it would. Tomorrow is all right; it carries in its grip good things as well as troubles. Bless my soul, when I sit down and think over the things which I once feared might possibly descend upon me, I laugh! Where are those feared things now? I don't know—have almost forgotten that I ever feared them.

You do not need to *fight* Worry—that isn't the way to overcome the habit. Just practice concentration, and then learn to concentrate upon something right before you, and you will find that the worry thought has vanished. The mind can think of but one thing at a time, and if you concentrate upon a bright thing, the other thing will fade away. There are better ways of overcoming objectionable thoughts than by fighting them. Learn to concentrate upon thoughts of an opposite character, and you will have solved the problem.

When the mind is full of worry thoughts, it cannot find time to work out plans to benefit you. But when you have concentrated upon bright, helpful thoughts, you will discover that it will start to work subconsciously; and when the time comes you will find all sorts of plans and methods by which you will be able to meet the demands upon you. Keep your mental attitude right, and all things will be added unto you. There's no sense in worrying; nothing has ever been gained by it, and nothing ever will be. Bright, cheerful and happy thoughts *attract* bright, cheerful and happy things to us—worry drives them away. Cultivate the right mental attitude.

CHAPTER VIII

The Law Of Mental Control

Your thoughts are either faithful servants or tyrannical masters—just as you allow them to be. You have the say about it; take your choice. They will either go about your work under direction of the firm will, doing it the best they know how, not only in your waking hours, but when you are asleep— some of our best mental work being performed for us when our conscious mentality is at rest, as is evidenced by the fact that when the morning comes we find troublesome problems have been worked out for us during the night, after we had dismissed them from our minds—apparently; or they will ride all over us and make us their slaves if we are foolish enough to allow them to do so. More than half the people of the world are slaves of every vagrant thought which may see fit to torment them.

Your mind is given you for your good and for your own use—not to use you. There are very few people who seem to realize this and who understand the art of managing the mind. The key to the mystery is Concentration. A little practice will develop within every man the power to use the mental machine properly. When you have some mental work to do concentrate upon it to the exclusion of everything else, and you will find that the mind will get right down to business—to the work at hand—and matters will be cleared up in no time. There is an absence of friction, and all waste motion or lost power is obviated. Every pound of energy is put to use, and every revolution of the mental driving-wheel counts for something. It pays to be able to be a competent mental engi-

neer.

And the man who understands how to run his mental engine knows that one of the important things is to be able to stop it when the work has been done. He does not keep putting coal in the furnace, and maintaining a high pressure after the work is finished, or when the day's portion of the work has been done, and the fires should be banked until the next day. Some people act as if the engine should be kept running whether there was any work to be done or not, and then they complain if it gets worn out and wobbles and needs repairing. These mental engines are fine machines, and need intelligent care.

To those who are acquainted with the laws of mental control it seems absurd for one to lie awake at night fretting about the problems of the day, or more often, of the morrow. It is just as easy to slow down the mind as it is to slow down an engine, and thousands of people are learning to do this in these days of New Thought. The best way to do it is to think of something else— as far different from the obtruding thought as possible. There is no use fighting an objectionable thought with the purpose of "downing" it; that is a great waste of energy, and the more you keep on saying, "I won't think of this thing!" the more it keeps on coming into your mind, for you are holding it there for the purpose of hitting it. Let it go; don't give it another thought; fix the mind on something entirely different, and keep the attention there by an effort of the will. A little practice will do much for you in this direction. There is only room for one thing at a time in the focus of attention; so put all your attention upon one thought, and the others will sneak off. Try it for yourself.

CHAPTER IX

Asserting The Life-force

I have spoken to you of the advantage of getting rid of Fear. Now I wish to put LIFE into you. Many of you have been going along as if you were dead— no ambition—no energy—no vitality— no interest—no life. This will never do. You are stagnating. Wake up and display a few signs of life! This is not the

place in which you can stalk around like a living corpse— this is the place for wide-awake, active, *live* people, and a good general awakening is what is needed; although it would take nothing less than a blast from Gabriel's trumpet to awaken some of the people who are stalking around thinking that they are alive, but who are really dead to all that makes life worth while.

We must let Life flow through us, and allow it to express itself naturally. Do not let the little worries of life, or the big ones either, depress you and cause you to lose your vitality. Assert the Life Force within you, and manifest it in every thought, act and deed, and before long you will be exhilarated and fairly bubbling over with vitality and energy.

Put a little life into your work—into your pleasures—into yourself. Stop doing things in a half-hearted way, and begin to take an interest in what you are doing, saying and thinking. It is astonishing how much interest we may find in the ordinary things of life, if we will only wake up. There are interesting things all around us—interesting events occurring every moment —but we will not be aware of them unless we assert our life force and begin to actually live instead of merely existing.

No man or woman ever amounted to anything unless he or she put life into the tasks of everyday life—the acts— the thoughts. What the world needs is live men and women. Just look into the eyes of the people whom you meet, and see how few of them are really *alive*. The most of them lack that expression of conscious life which distinguishes the man who *lives* from the one who simply *exists.*

I want you to acquire this sense of conscious life so that you may manifest it in your life and show what Mental Science has done for you. I want you to get to work today and begin to make yourselves over according to the latest pattern. You can do this if you will only take the proper interest in the task.

Affirmation And Exercise

"I Am Alive."

Fix in your mind the thought that the "I" within you is very much alive and that you are manifesting life fully, mentally and physically. And keep this thought there, aiding yourself with constant repetitions of the watchword. Don't let the thought escape you, but keep pushing it back into the mind. Keep it before the mental vision as much as possible. Repeat the watchword when you awaken in the morning—say it when you retire at night. And say it at meal times, and whenever else you can during the day—at least once an hour. Form the mental picture of yourself as filled with Life and Energy. Live up to it as far as possible. When you start in to perform a task say "I Am Alive" and mix up as much life as possible in the task. If you find yourself feeling depressed, say "I Am Alive," and then take a few deep breaths, and with each inhalation let the mind hold the thought that you are breathing in Strength and Life, and as you exhale, hold the thought that you are breathing out all the old, dead, negative conditions and are glad to get rid of them. Then finish up with an earnest, vigorous affirmation: "I Am Alive," and *mean* it when you say it, too.

And let your thoughts take form in action. Don't rest content with merely saying that you are alive, but prove it with your acts. Take an interest in doing things, and don't go around "mooning" or day-dreaming. Get down to business, and LIVE.

CHAPTER X

Training The Habit-mind

Professor William James, the well-known teacher of, and writer upon Psychology, very truly says:

"The great thing in all education is to make our nervous system our ally instead of our enemy. For this we must make automatic and habitual, as early as possible, as many useful actions as we can, and as carefully guard against growing into ways that are likely to be disadvantageous. In the acquisition of a new habit, or the leaving off of an old one, we must take care to launch ourselves with as strong and decided initiative as possible. Never suffer an exception to occur until the new habit is securely rooted in your life. Seize the very first possible opportunity to act on every resolution you make and on every emotional prompting you may experience, in the direction of the habits you aspire to gain."

This advice is along the lines familiar to all students of Mental Science, but it states the matter more plainly than the majority of us have done. It impresses upon us the importance of passing on to the subconscious mind the proper impulses, so that they will become automatic and "second nature." Our subconscious mentality is a great store house for all sorts of suggestions from ourselves and others, and, as it is the "habit-mind," we must be careful to send it the proper material from which it may make habits. If we get into the habit of doing certain things, we may be sure that the subconscious mentality will make it easier for us to do just the same thing over and over again, easier each time, until finally we are firmly bound with the ropes and chains of the habit, and find it more or less difficult, sometimes almost impossible, to free ourselves from the hateful thing.

We should cultivate good habits against the hour of need. The time will come when we will be required to put forth our best efforts, and it rests with us today whether that hour of need shall find us doing the proper thing automatically and almost without thought, or struggling to do it bound down and hindered with the chains of things opposed to that which we desire at that moment.

We must be on guard at all times to prevent the forming of undesirable habits. There may be no special harm in doing a certain thing today, or perhaps again tomorrow, but there may be much harm in setting up *the habit* of doing that particular thing. If you are confronted with the question: "Which of these two things should I do?" the best answer is: "I will do that which I would like to become a habit with me."

In forming a new habit, or in breaking an old one, we should throw ourselves into the task with as much enthusiasm as possible, in order to gain the most ground before the energy expends itself when it meets with friction from the opposing habits already formed. We should start in by making as strong an impression as possible upon the subconscious mentality. Then we should be constantly on guard against temptations to break the new resolution "just this once." This "just once" idea kills off more good resolutions than any other one cause. The moment you yield "just this once," you introduce the thin edge of the wedge that will, in the end, split your resolution into pieces.

Equally important is the fact that each time you resist temptation the stronger does your resolution become. Act upon your resolution as early and as often as possible, as with every manifestation of thought in action, the stronger does it become. You are adding to the strength of your original resolution every time you back it up with action.

The mind has been likened to a piece of paper that has been folded. Ever afterwards it has a tendency to fold in the same crease—unless we make a new crease or fold, when it will follow the last lines. And the creases are habits—every time we make one it is so much easier for the mind to fold along the same crease afterward. Let us make our mental creases in the right direction.

CHAPTER XI

The Psychology Of Emotion

One is apt to think of the emotions as independent from habit. We easily may think of one acquiring habits of action, and even of thinking, but we are apt to regard the emotions as something connected with "feeling" and quite divorced from intellectual effort. Yet, notwithstanding the distinction between the two, both are dependent largely upon habit, and one may repress, increase, develop, and change one's emotions, just as one may regulate habits of action and lines of thought.

It is an axiom of psychology that "Emotions deepen by repetition." If a person allows a state of feeling to thoroughly take possession of him, he will find it easier to yield to the same emotion the second time, and so on, until the particular emotion or feeling becomes second nature to him. If an undesirable emotion shows itself inclined to take up a permanent abode with you, you had better start to work to get rid of it, or at least to master it. And the best time to do this is at the start; for each repetition renders the habit more firmly intrenched, and the task of dislodging it more difficult.

Were you ever jealous? If so, you will remember how insidious was its first approach, how subtly it whispered hateful suggestions into your willing ear, and how gradually it followed up such suggestions, until, finally you began to see green. (Jealousy has an effect upon the bile, and causes it to poison the blood. This is why the idea of green is always associated with it.) Then you will remember how the thing seemed to grow, taking possession of you until you scarcely could shake it off. You found it much easier to become jealous the next time. It seemed to bring before you all sorts of objects apparently justifying your suspicions and feeling. Everything began to look green—the greeneyed monster waxed fat.

And so it is with every feeling or emotion. If you give way to a fit of rage, you will find it easier to become angry the next time, on less provocation. The habit of feeling and acting "mean" does not take long to firmly settle itself in its new home if encouraged. Worry is a great habit for growing and waxing fat. People start by worrying about big things, and then begin to worry and fret about some smaller thing. And then the merest trifle worries and distresses them. They imagine that all sorts of evil things are about to befall them. If they start on a journey they are certain there is going to be a wreck. If a telegram comes, it is sure to contain some dreadful tidings. If a child seems a little quiet, the worrying mother is positive it is going to fall ill and die. If the husband seems thoughtful, as he revolves some business plan in his mind, then the good wife is convinced that he is beginning to cease to love her, and indulges in a crying spell. And so it goes—worry, worry, worry—each indulgence making the habit more at home. After a while the continued thought shows itself in action. Not only is the mind poisoned

by the blue thoughts, but the forehead shows deep lines between the eyebrows, and the voice takes on that whining, rasping tone so common among worry-burdened people.

The condition of mind known as "fault-finding" is another emotion that grows fat with exercise. First, fault is found with this thing, then with that, and finally with everything. The person becomes a chronic "nagger"—a burden to friends and relatives, and a thing to be avoided by outsiders. Women make the greatest naggers. Not because men are any better, but simply because a man nagger is apt to have the habit knocked out of him by other men who will not stand his nonsense—he finds that he is making things too hot for himself, and he reforms; while a woman has more of a chance to indulge in the habit. But this nagging is all a matter of habit. It grows from small beginnings, and each time it is indulged in it throws out another root, branch, or tendril, and fastens itself the closer to the one who has given it soil in which to grow.

Envy, uncharitableness, gossip, scandal-mongering, are all habits of this kind. The seeds are in every human breast, and only need good soil and a little watering to become lusty and strong.

Each time you give way to one of these negative emotions, the easier do you make it for a recurrence of the same thing, or similar ones. Sometimes by encouraging one unworthy emotion, you find that you have given room for the growth of a whole family of these mental weeds.

Now, this is not a good old orthodox preach ment against the sin of bad thoughts. It is merely a calling of your attention to the law underlying the psychology of emotions. Nothing new about it—old as the hills—so old that many of us have forgotten all about it.

If you wish to manifest these constantly disagreeable and unpleasant traits, and to suffer the unhappiness that comes from them, by all means do so—that is your own business, and privilege. It's none of mine, and I am not preaching at you —it keeps me busy minding my own business and keeping an eye on

my own undesirable habits and actions. I am merely telling you the law regarding the matter, and you may do the rest. If you wish to choke out these habits, there are two ways open to you. First, whenever you find yourself indulging in a negative thought or feeling, take right hold of it and say to it firmly, and vigorously, "Get out!" It won't like this at first, and will bridle up, curve its back and snarl like an offended cat. But never mind—just say "Scat" to it. The next time it will not be so confident and aggressive—it will have manifested a little of the fear-habit. Each time you repress and choke out a tendency of this kind, the weaker it will become, and the stronger will your will be.

Professor James says: "Refuse to express a passion, and it dies. Count ten before venting your anger, and its occasion seems ridiculous. Whistling to keep up courage is no mere figure of speech. On the other hand, sit all day in a moping posture, sigh, and reply to everything with a dismal voice, and your melancholy lingers. There is no more valuable precept in moral education than this, as all who have experience know: if we wish to conquer emotional tendencies in ourselves, we must assiduously, and in the first instance, cold-bloodedly, go through the *outward movements* of those contrary dispositions which we prefer to cultivate. Smooth the brow, brighten the eye, contract the dorsal rather than the ventral aspect of the frame, and speak in a major key, pass the genial compliment, and your heart must be frigid indeed if it does not gradually thaw." CHAPTER XII

Developing New Brain-cells

I have spoken of the plan of getting rid of undesirable states of feeling by driving them out. But a far better way is to cultivate the feeling or emotion directly opposed to the one you wish to eradicate.

We are very apt to regard ourselves as the reatures of our emotions and feelings, and to fancy that these feelings and emotions are "we." But such is far from being the truth. It is true that the majority of the race are slaves of their emotions and feelings, and are governed by them to a great degree. They think that feelings are things that rule one and from which one cannot free himself, and so they cease to rebel. They yield to the feeling without question, although they may know that the emotion or mental trait is calculated to injure them, and to bring unhappiness and failure instead of happiness and success. They say "we are made that way," and let it go at that.

The new Psychology is teaching the people better things. It tells them that they are masters of their emotions and feelings, instead of being their slaves. It tells them that brain-cells may be developed that will manifest along desirable lines, and that the old brain-cells that have been manifesting so unpleasantly may be placed on the retired list, and allowed to atrophy from want of use. People may make themselves over, and change their entire natures. This is not mere idle theory, but is a working fact which has been demonstrated by thousands of people, and which is coming more and more before the attention of the race.

No matter what theory of mind we entertain, we must admit that the brain is the organ and instrument of the mind, in our present state of existence, at least, and that the brain must be considered in this matter. The brain is like a wonderful musical instrument, having millions of keys, upon which we may play innumerable combinations of sounds. We come into the world with certain tendencies, temperaments, and predispositions. We may account for these tendencies by heredity, or we may account for them upon theories of pre-existence, but the facts remain the same. Certain keys seem to respond to our touch more easily than others. Certain notes seem to sound forth as the current of circumstances sweeps over the strings. And certain other notes are less easily vibrated. But we find that if we but make an effort of the will to restrain the utterance of some of these easily sounded strings, they will grow more difficult to sound, and less liable to be stirred by the passing breeze. And if we will pay attention to some of the other strings that have

not been giving forth a clear tone, we will soon get them in good workig order; their notes will chime forth clear and vibrant, and will drown the less pleasant sounds. We have millions of unused brain-cells awaiting our cultivation. We are using but a few of them, and some of these we are working to death. We are able to give some of these cells a rest, by using other cells. The brain may be trained and cultivated in a manner incredible to one who has not looked into the subject. Mental attitudes may be acquired and cultivated, changed and discarded, at will. There is no longer any excuse for people manifesting unpleasant and harmful mental states. We have the remedy in our own hands.

We acquire habits of thought, feeling, and action, by repeated use. We may be born with a tendency in a certain direction, or we may acquire tendencies by suggestions from others; such as the examples of those around us, suggestions from reading, listening to teachers. We are a bundle of mental habits. Each time we indulge in an undesirable thought or habit, the easier does it become to repeat that thought or action. And the oftener we give forth a certain desirable thought, or perform a desirable action, the easier does it become for us to repeat that thought or action.

Mental scientists are in the habit of speaking of desirable thoughts or mental attitudes as "positive," and of the undesirable ones as "negative." There is a good reason for this. The mind instinctively recognizes certain things as good for the individual to which it belongs, and it clears the path for such thoughts, and interposes the least resistance to them. They have a much greater effect than an undesirable thought possesses, and one positive thought will counteract a number of negative thoughts. The best way to overcome undesirable or negative thoughts and feelings is to cultivate the positive ones. The positive thought is the strongest plant, and will in time starve out the negative one by withdrawing from it the nourishment necessary for its existence.

Of course the negative thought will set up a vigorous resistance at first, for it is a fight for life with it. In the slang words of the time, it "sees its finish" if the positive thought is allowed to grow and develop; and, consequently, it makes things unpleasant for the individual until he has started well into the work of starving it out. Brain cells do not like to be laid on the shelf any more than does any other form of living energy, and they rebel and struggle until they become too weak to do so. The best way is to pay as little attention as possible to these weeds of the mind, but put in as much time as possible watering, caring for and attending to the new and beautiful plants in the garden of the mind.

For instance, if you are apt to hate people, you can best overcome the negative thought by cultivating Love in its place. Think Love, and act it out, as often as possible. Cultivate thoughts of kindness, and act as kindly as you can to everyone with whom you come in contact. You will have trouble at the start, but gradually Love will master Hate, and the latter will begin to droop and wither. If you have a tendency toward the "blues" cultivate a smile, and a cheerful view of things. Insist upon your mouth wearing upturned corners, and make an effort of the will to look upon the bright side of things. The "bluedevils" will set up a fight, of course, but pay no attention to them— just go on cultivating optimism and cheerfulness. Let "Bright, Cheerful and Happy" be your watchword, *and try to live it out.*

These recipes may seem very old and timeworn, but they are psychological truths and may be used by you to advantage. If you once comprehend the nature of the thing, the affirmations and autosuggestions of the several schools may be understood and taken advantage of. You may make yourself energetic instead of slothful, active instead of lazy, by this method. It is all a matter of practice and steady work. New Thought people often have much to say about "holding the thought;" and, indeed, it is necessary to "hold the thought" in order to accomplish results. But something more is needed. You must "act out" the thought until it becomes a fixed habit with you. Thoughts take form in action; and in turn actions influence thought. So by "acting out" certain lines of thought, the actions react upon the mind, and increase the development of the part of the mind having close relation to the act. Each time the mind entertains a thought, the easier becomes the resulting action—and each time an act is performed, the easier becomes the corresponding thought. So you see the thing works both ways—action and reaction. If you feel cheerful and happy, it is very natural for you to laugh. And if you will laugh a little, you will begin to feel bright and cheerful. Do you see what I am trying to get at? Here it is, in a nutshell: // *you wish to cultivate a certain habit of action, begin by cultivating the mental attitude corresponding to it. And as a means of cultivating that mental attitude, start in to "act-out," or go through, the motions of the act corresponding to the thought.* Now, see if you cannot apply this rule. Take up something that you really feel should be done, but which you do not *feel* like doing. Cultivate the thought leading up to it—say to yourself: "I like to do so and so," and then go through the motions (cheerfully, remember!) and act out the thought that you like to do the thing. Take an interest in the doing—study out the best way to do it—put brains into it—take a pride in it—and you will find yourself doing the thing with a considerable amount of pleasure and interest— you will have cultivated a new habit.

If you prefer trying it on some mental trait of which you wish to be rid, it will work the same way. Start in to cultivate the opposite trait, and think it out and act it out for all you are worth. Then watch the change that will come over you. Don't be discouraged at the resistance you will encounter at first, but sing gaily: "I Can and I Will," and get to work in earnest. The important thing in this work is to keep cheerful and interested. If you manage to do this, the rest will be easy.

CHAPTER XIII

The Attractive Power—Desire Force.

We have discussed the necessity of getting rid of fear, that your desire may have full strength with which to work. Supposing that you have mastered this part of the task, or at least started on the road to mastery, I will now call your attention to another important branch of the subject. I allude to the subject of mental leaks. No, I don't mean the leakage arising from your failure to keep your own secrets—that is also important, but forms another story. The leakage I am now referring to is that occasioned by the habit of having the attention attracted to and distracted by every passing fancy.

In order to attain a thing it is necessary that the mind should fall in love with it, and be conscious of its existence, almost to the exclusion of everything else. You must get in love with the thing you wish to attain, just as much as you would if you were to meet the girl or man you wished to marry. I do not mean that you should become a monomaniac upon the subject, and should lose all interest in everything else in the world—that won't do, for the mind must have recreation and change. But, I do mean that you must be so "set" upon the desired thing that all else will seem of secondary importance. A man in love may be pleasant to every one else, and may go through the duties and pleasures of life with good spirit, but underneath it all he is humming to himself "Just One Girl;" and every one of his actions is bent toward getting that girl, and making a comfortable home for her. Do you see what I mean? You must get in love with the thing you want, and you must get in love with it in earnest—none of this latter-day flirting, "on-today and off-tomorrow" sort of love, but the good old-fashioned kind, that used to make it impossible for a young man to get to sleep unless he took a walk around his best girl's house, just to be sure it was still there. That's the real kind!

And the man or woman in search of success must make of that desired thing his ruling passion—he must keep his mind on the main chance. Success is jealous—that's why we speak of her as feminine. She demands a man's whole affection, and if he begins flirting with other fair charmers, she soon turns her back upon him. If a man allows his strong interest in the main chance to be sidetracked, he will be the loser. Mental Force operates best when it is concentrated. You must give to the desired thing your best and most earnest thought. Just as the man who is thoroughly in love will think out plans and schemes whereby he may please the fair one, so will the man who is in love with his work or business give it his best thought, and the result will be that a hundred and one plans will come into his field of consciousness, many of which are very important. The mind works on the subconscious plane, remember, and almost always along the lines of the ruling passion or desire. It will fix up things, and patch together plans and schemes, and when you need them the most it will pop them into your consciousness, and you will feel like hurrahing, just as if you had received some valuable aid from outside.

But if you scatter your thought-force, the subconscious mind will not know just how to please you, and the result is that you are apt to be put off from this source of aid and assistance. Beside this, you will miss the powerful result of concentrated thought in the conscious working out of the details of your plans. And then again the man whose mind is full of a dozen interests fails to exert the attracting power that is manifested by the man of the one ruling passion, and he fails to draw to him persons, things, and results that will aid in the working out of his plans, and will also fail to place himself in the current of attraction whereby he is brought into contact with those who will be glad to help him because of harmonious interests.

I have noticed, in my own affairs, that when I would allow myself to be sidetracked by anything outside of my regular line of work, it would be only a short time before my receipts dropped off, and my business showed signs of a lack of vitality. Now, many may say that this was because I left undone some things that I would have done if my mind had been centered on the business. This is true; but I have noticed like results in cases where there was nothing to be *done*—cases in which the seed was sown, and the crop was awaited. And, in just such cases, as soon as I directed my thought to the matter the seed began to sprout. I do not mean that I had to send out great mental waves with the idea of affecting people—not a bit of it. I simply began to realize what a good thing I had, and how much people wanted it, and how glad they would be to know of it, and all that sort of thing, and lo! my thought seemed to vitalize the work, and the seed began to sprout. This is no mere fancy, for I have experienced it on several occasions; I have spoken to many others on the subject, and I find that our experiences tally perfectly. So don't get into the habit of permitting these mental leaks. Keep your Desire fresh and active, and let it get in its work without interference from conflicting desires. Keep in love with the thing you wish to attain—feed your fancy with it—see it as accomplished already, *but don't lose your interest.* Keep your eye on the main chance, and keep your one ruling passion strong and vigorous. Don't be a mental polygamist—one mental love is all that a man needs—that is, *one at a time.*

Some scientists have claimed that something that might as well be called "Love" is at the bottom of the whole of life. They claim that the love of the plant for water causes it to send forth its roots until the loved thing is found. They say that the love of the flower for the sun, causes it to grow away from the dark places, so that it may receive the light. The so-called "chemical affinities" are really a form of love. And Desire is a manifestation of this Universal Life Love. So I am not using a mere figure of speech when I tell you that you must love the thing you wish to attain. Nothing but intense love will enable you to surmount the many obstacles placed in your path. Nothing but that love will enable you to bear the burdens of the task. The more Desire you

have for a thing, the more you Love it; and the more you Love it, the greater will be the attractive force exerted toward its attainment—both within yourself, and outside of you. So love but one thing at a time—don't be a mental Mormon.

CHAPTER XIV
The Great Dynamic Forces
You have noticed the difference between the successful and strong men in any walk of life, and the unsuccessful weak men around them. You are conscious of the widely differing characteristics of the two classes, but somehow find it difficult to express just in what the difference lies. Let us take a look at the matter.

Buxton said: "The longer I live, the more certain I am that the great difference between men, the feeble and the powerful, the great and the insignificant, is energy and invincible determination—a purpose once fixed and then Death or Victory. That quality will do anything that can be done in this world—and no talents, no circumstances, no opportunities will make a twolegged creature a man without it." I do not see how the idea could be more clearly expressed than Buxton has spoken. He has put his finger right in the center of the subject—his eye has seen into the heart of it.

Energy and invincible determination—these two things will sweep away mighty barriers, and will surmount the greatest obstacles. And yet they must be used together. Energy without determination will go to waste. Lots of men have plenty of energy—they are full to overflowing with it; and yet they lack concentration—they lack the concentrated force that enables them to bring their power to bear upon the right spot. Energy is not nearly so rare a thing as many imagine it to be. I can look around me at any time, and pick out a number of people I know who are full of energy—many of them are energy *plus*—and yet, somehow, they do not seem to make any headway. They are wasting jtheir energy all the time. Now they are fooling with this thing—now meddling with that. They will take up

some trifling thing of no real interest or importance, and waste enough energy and nervous force to carry them through a hard day's work; and yet when they are through, nothing has been accomplished.

Others who have plenty of energy, fail to direct it by the power of the Will toward the desired end. "Invincible determination"—those are the words. Do they not thrill you with their power? If you have something to do, get to work and do it. Marshal your energy, and then guide and direct it by your Will—bestow upon it that "invincible determination" and you will do the thing.

Everyone has within him a giant will, but the majority of us are too lazy to use it. We cannot get ourselves nerved up to the point at which we can say, truthfully: *"/ Will."* If we can but screw up our courage to that point, and will then pin it in place so that it will not slip back, we will be able to call into play that wonderful power—the Human Will. Man, as a rule, has but the faintest conception of the power of the Will, but those who have studied along the occult teachings, know that the Will is one of the great dynamic forces of the universe, and if harnessed and directed properly it is capable of accomplishing almost miraculous things.

"Energy and Invincible Determination"— aren't they magnificent words? Commit them to memory—press them like a die into the wax of your mind, and they will be a constant inspiration to you in hours of need. If you can get these words to vibrating in your being, you will be a giant among pygmies. Say these words over and over again, and see how you are filled with new life— see how your blood will circulate — how your nerves will tingle. Make these words a part of yourself, and then go forth anew to the battle of life, encouraged and strengthened. Put them into practice. "Energy and Invincible Determination"—let that be your motto in your work-a-day life, and you will be one of those rare men who are able to "do things."

Many persons are deterred from doing their best by the fact that they underrate themselves by comparison with the successful ones of life, or rather, overrate the successful ones by comparison with themselves.

One of the curious things noticed by those who are brought in contact with the people who have "arrived" is the fact that these successful people are not extraordinary after all. You meet with some great writer, and you are disappointed to find him very ordinary indeed. He does not converse brilliantly, and, in fact, you know a score of everyday people who seem far more brilliant than this man who dazzles you by his brightness in his books. You meet some great statesman, and he does not seem nearly so wise as lots of old fellows in your own village, who waste their wisdom upon the desert air. You meet some great captain of industry, and he does not give you the impression of the shrewdness so marked in some little bargain-driving trader in your own town. How is this, anyway? Are the reputations of these people fictitious, or what is the trouble?

The trouble is this: You have imagined these people to be made of superior metal, and are disappointed to find them made of the same stuff as yourself and those about you. But, you ask, wherein does their greatness of achievement lie? Chiefly in this: Belief in themselves and in their inherent power, in their faculty to concentrate on the work in hand, when they are working, and in their ability to prevent leaks of power when they are not working. *They believe in themselves,* and make every effort count. Your village wiseman spills his wisdom on every corner, and talks to a lot of fools; when if he really were wise he would save up his wisdom and place it where it would do some work. The brilliant writer does not waste his wit upon every comer; in fact, he shuts the drawer in which he contains his wit, and opens it only when he is ready to concentrate and get down to business.

The captain of industry has no desire to impress you with his shrewdness and "smartness." He never did, even when he was young. While his companions were talking and boasting, and "blow-ing," this future successful financier was "sawin' wood and sayin' nuthin'."

The great people of the woild—that is, those who have "arrived"—are not very different from you, or me, or the rest of us—all of us are about the same at the base. You have only to meet them to see how very "ordinary" they are, after all. But, don't forget the fact that *they* know how to use the material that is in them; while the rest of the crowd does not, and, in fact, even doubts whether the true stuff is there. The man or woman who "gets there," usually starts out by realizing that he or she is not so very different, after all, from the successful people that they hear so much about. This gives them confidence, and the result is they find out that they are able to "do things." Then they learn to keep their mouths closed, and to avoid wasting and dissipating their energy. They store up energy, and concentrate it upon the task at hand; while their companions are scattering their energies in every direction, trying to show off and let people know how smart they are. The man or woman who "gets there," prefers to wait for the applause that follows deeds accomplished, and cares very little for the praise that attends promises of what we expect to do "some day," or an exhibition of "smartness" without works.

One of the reasons that people who are thrown in with successful men often manifest success themselves, is that they are able to watch the successful man and sort of "catch the trick" of his greatness. They see that he is an everyday sort of man, but that he thoroughly believes in himself, and also that he does not waste energy, but reserves all his force for the actual tasks before him. And, profiting by example, they start to work and put the lesson into practice in their own lives.

Now what is the moral of this talk? Simply this: Don't undervalue yourself, or overvalue others. Realize that you are made of good stuff, and that locked within your mind are many good things. Then get to work and unfold those good things, and make something out of that good stuff. Do this by attention to the things before you, and by giving to each the best that is in you, knowing that plenty of more good things are in you ready for the fresh tasks that will come. Put the best of yourself into the undertaking on hand, and do not cheat the present task in favor of some future one. Your supply is inexhaustible. And don't waste your good stuff on the crowd of gapers, watchers and critics who are standing around watching you work. Save your good stuff for your job, and don't be in too much of a hurry for applause. Save up your good thoughts for "copy" if you are a writer; save up your bright schemes for actual practice, if you are a business man; save up your wisdom for occasion, if you are a statesman; and, in each case, avoid the desire to scatter your pearls before—well, before the gaping crowd that wants to be entertained by a "free show."

Nothing very "high" about this teaching, perhaps, but it is what many of you need very much. Stop fooling, and get down to business. Stop wasting good raw material, and start to work making something worth while.

CHAPTER XV

Claiming Your Own

In a recent conversation, I was telling a woman to pluck up courage and to reach out for a certain good thing for which she had been longing for many years, and which, at last, appeared to be in sight. I told her that it looked as if her desire was about to be gratified—that the Law of Attraction was bringing it to her. She lacked faith, and kept on repeating, "Oh! it's too good to be true—it's too good for *me!*" She had not emerged from the worm-of-the-dust stage, and although she was in sight of the Promised Land she refused to enter it because it "was too *good* for her." I think I succeeded in putting sufficient "ginger" into her to enable her to claim her own, for the last reports indicate that she is taking possession.

But that is not what I wish to tell you. I want to call your attention to the fact that nothing is too good for You—no matter how great the thing may be—no matter how undeserving you may seem to be. You are entitled to the best there is, for it is your direct inheritance. So don't be afraid to ask—demand—and take. The good things of the world are not the portion of any favored sons. They belong to all, but they come only to those who are wise enough to recognize that the good things are theirs by right, and who are sufficiently courageous to reach out for them. Many good things are lost for want of the asking. Many splendid things are lost to you because of your feeling that you are unworthy of them. Many great things are lost to you because you lack the confidence and courage to demand and take possession of them.

"None but the brave deserves the fair," says the old adage, and the rule is true in all lines of human effort. If you keep on repeating that you are unworthy of the good thing—that it is too good for you—the Law will be apt to take you at your word and believe what you say. That's a peculiar thing about the Law— it believes what you say—it takes you in earnest. So beware what you say to it, for it will be apt to give credence. Say to it that you are worthy of the best there is, and that there is nothing too good for you, and you will be likely to have the Law take you in earnest, and say, "I guess he is right; I'm going to give him the whole bakeshop if he wants it—he knows his rights, and what's the use of trying to deny it to him?" But if you say, "Oh, it's too good for *me!*" the Law will probably say, "Well, I wouldn't wonder but what that is so. Surely he ought to know, and it isn't for me to contradict him." And so it goes.

Why should anything be too good for you? Did you ever stop to think just what you are? You are a manifestation of the Whole Thing, and have a perfect right to all there is. Or, if you prefer it this way, you are a child of the Infinite, and are heir to it all. You are telling the truth in either statement, or both. At any rate, no matter for what you ask, you are merely demanding your own. And the more in earnest you are about demanding it—the more confident you are of receiving it—the more will you use in reaching out for it—the surer you will be to obtain it.

Strong desire—confident expectation—courage in action—these things bring to you your own. But before you put these forces into effect, you must awaken to a realization that you are merely asking for your own, and not for something to which you have no right or claim. So long as there exists in your mind the last sneaking bit of doubt as to your right to the things you want, you will be setting up a resistance to the operation of the Law. You may demand as vigorously as you please, but you will lack the courage to act, if you have a lingering doubt of your right to the thing you want. If you persist in regarding the desired thing as if it belonged to another, instead of to yourself, you will be placing yourself in the position of the covetous or envious man, or even in the position of a tempted thief. In such a case your mind will revolt at proceeding with the work, for it instinctively will recoil from the idea of taking what is not your own— the mind is honest. But when you realize that the best the Universe holds belongs to you as a Divine Heir, and that there is enough for all without your robbing anyone else; then the friction is removed, and the barrier broken down, and the Law proceeds to do its work.

I do not believe in this "humble" business. This meek and lowly attitude does not appeal to me—there is no sense in it, at all. The idea of making a virtue of such things, when Man is the heir of the Universe, and is entitled to whatever he needs for his growth, happiness and satisfaction! I do not mean that one should assume a blustering and domineering attitude of mind— that is also absurd, for true strength does not so exhibit itself. The blusterer is a self-confessed weakling—he blusters to disguise his weakness. The truly strong man is calm, self-contained, and carries with him a consciousness of strength which renders unnecessary the bluster and fuss of assumed strength. But get away from this hypnotism of "humility"—this "meek and lowly" attitude of mind. Remember the horrible example of Uriah Heep, and beware of imitating him. Throw back your head, and look

the world square in the face. There's nothing to be afraid of—the world is apt to be as much afraid of you, as you are of it, anyway. Be a man, or woman, and not a crawling thing. And this applies to your mental attitude, as well as to your outward demeanor. Stop this crawling in your mind. See yourself as standing erect and facing life without fear, and you will gradually grow into your ideal.

There is nothing that is too good for you— not a thing. The best there is, is not beginning to be good enough for you; for there are still better things ahead. The best gift that the world has to offer is a mere bauble compared to the great things in the Cosmos that await your coming of age. So don't be afraid to reach out for these playthings of life—these baubles of this plane of consciousness. Reach out for them— grab a whole fistful— play with them until you are tired; that's what they are made for, anyway. They are made for our express use—not to look at, but to be played with, if you desire. Help yourself— there's a whole shopful of these toys awaiting your desire, demand and taking. Don't be bashful! Don't let me hear any more of this silly talk about things being too good for you. Pshaw! You have been like the Emperor's little son thinking that the tin soldiers and toy drum were far too good for him, and refusing to reach out for them. But you don't find this trouble with children as a rule. They instinctively recognize that nothing is too good for them. They want all that is in sight to play with, and they seem to feel that the things are theirs by right. And that is the condition of mind that we seekers after the Divine Adventure must cultivate. Unless we become as little children we cannot enter the Kingdom of Heaven.

The things we see around us are the playthings of the Kindergarten of God, playthings which we use in our game-tasks. Help yourself to them—ask for them without bashfulness—demand as many as you can make use of—they are yours. And if you don't see just what you want, ask for it—there's a big reserve stock on the shelves, and in the closets. Play, play, play, to your heart's content. Learn to weave mats— to build houses with the blocks—to stitch out-lines on the squares—play the game through, and play it well. And demand all the proper materials for the play—don't be bashful—there's enough to go round.

But—remember this! While all this be true, the best things are still only game-things—toys, blocks, mats, cubes, and all the rest. Useful, most use-ful for the learning of the lessons—pleasant, most pleasant with which to play—and desirable, most desirable, for these purposes. Get all the fun and prof-it out of the use of things that is pos-sible. Throw yourself heartily into the game, and play it out—it is Good. But, here's the thing to remember—never lose sight of the fact that these good things are but playthings— part of the game—and you must be perfectly will-ing to lay them aside when the time comes to pass into the next class, and not cry and mourn because you must leave your playthings behind you. Do not allow yourself to become unduly at-tached to them—they are for your use and pleasure, but are not a part of you—not essential to your happiness in the next stage. Despise them not because of their lack of Reality—they are great things relatively, and you may as well have all the fun out of them that you can—don't be a spiritual prig, standing aside and refusing to join in the game. But do not tie yourself to them—they are good to use and play with, but not good enough to use *you* and to make *you* a plaything. Don't let the toys turn the tables on you.

This is the difference between the Master of Circumstances and the Slave of Circumstances. The Slave thinks that these playthings are real, and that he is not good enough to have them. He gets only a few toys, because he is afraid to ask for more, and he misses most of the fun. And then, considering the toys to be real, and not realizing that there are plenty more where these came from, he attaches himself to the little trinkets that have come his way, and allows him-self to be made a slave of them. He is afraid that they may be taken away from him, and he is afraid to toddle across the floor and help himself to the others. The Master knows that all are his for the asking. He demands that which he needs from day to day, and does not worry about overloading himself; for he knows that there are "lots more," and that he cannot be cheated out of them. He plays, and plays well, and has a good time in the play—and he learns his Kin-dergarten lessons in the playing. But he does not become too much attached to his toys. He is willing to fling away the worn-out one, and reach out for a new one. And when he is called into the next room for promotion, he drops on the floor the worn-out toys of the day, and with glistening eyes and confident attitude of mind, marches into the next room—into the Great Unknown—with a smile on his face. He is not afraid, for he hears the voice of the Teacher, and knows that she is there waiting for him—in that Great Next Room.

CHAPTER XVI

Law, Not Chance

Some time ago I was talking to a man about the Attractive Power of Thought. He said that he did not believe that Thought could attract anything to him, and that it was all a matter of luck. He had found, he said, that ill luck relent-lessly pursued him, and that everything he touched went wrong. It always had, and always would, and he had grown to expect it. When he undertook a new thing he knew beforehand that it would go wrong and that no good would come of it. Oh, no! there wasn't anything in the theory of Attractive Thought, so far as he could see; it was all a matter of luck!

This man failed to see that by his own confession he was giving a most con-vincing argument in favor of the Law of Attraction. He was testifying that he was always expecting things to go wrong, and that they always came about as he expected. He was a magnificent illustration of the Law of Attraction—but he didn't know it, and no argument seemed to make the matter clear to him. He was "up against it," and there was no way out of it—he always expected the ill luck, and every occurrence proved that he was right, and that the Mental Science position was all nonsense.

There are many people who seem to think that the only way in which the Law of Attraction operates is when one *wishes* hard, strong and steady. They do not seem to realize that a strong *belief* is as efficacious as a strong wish. The suc-cessful man believes in himself and in his ultimate success, and, paying no at-tention to little setbacks, stumbles, tum-bles and slips, presses on eagerly to the goal, believing all the time that he will get there. His views and aims may al-ter as he progresses, and he may change his plans or have them changed for him, but all the time he knows in his heart that he will eventually "get there." He is not steadily *wishing* he may get there—he simply *feels* it and *believes* it, and thereby sets into operation the strongest forces known in the world of thought.

The man who just as steadily believes he is going to fail will invariably fail. How could he help it? There is no spe-cial miracle about it. Everything he does, thinks and says is tinctured with the thought of failure. Other people catch his spirit, and fail to trust him or his ability, which occurrences he in turn sets down as but other exhibitions of his ill luck, instead of ascribing them to his belief and expectation of failure. He is suggesting failure to himself all the time, and he invariably takes on the ef-fect of the autosuggestion. Then, again, he by his negative thoughts shuts up that portion of his mind from which should come the ideas and plans conducive to success and which do come to the man who is expecting success because he be-lieves in it. A state of discouragement is not the one in which bright ideas come to us. It is only when we are enthused and hopeful that our minds work out the bright ideas which we may turn to ac-count.

Men instinctively feel the atmosphere of failure hovering around certain of their fellows, and on the other hand rec-ognize something about others which leads them to say, when they hear of a temporary mishap befalling such a one: "Oh, he'll come out all right some-how—you can't down *him.*" It is the atmosphere caused by the prevailing Mental Attitude. Clear up your Mental Atmosphere!

There is no such thing as chance. Law maintains everywhere, and all that happens happens because of the operation of Law. You cannot name the simplest thing that ever occurred by chance—try it, and then run the thing down to a final analysis, and you will see it as the result of Law. It is as plain as mathematics. Plan and purpose; cause and effect. From the movements of worlds to the growth of the grain of mustard seed—all the result of Law. The fall of the stone down the mountain-side is not chance— forces which had been in operation for centuries caused it. And back of that cause were other causes, and so on until the Causeless Cause is reached.

And Life is not the result of chance— the Law is here, too. The Law is in full operation whether you know it or not— whether you believe in it or not. You may be the ignorant object upon which the Law operates, and bring yourself all sorts of trouble because of your ignorance of or opposition to the Law. Or you may fall in with the operations of the Law—get into its current, as it were—and Life will seem a far different thing to you. You cannot get outside of the Law, by refusing to have anything to do with it. You are at liberty to oppose it and produce all the friction you wish to—it doesn't hurt the Law, and you may keep it up until you learn your lesson.

The Law of Thought Attraction is one name for the Law, or rather for one manifestation of it. Again I say, your thoughts are real things. They go forth from you in all directions, combining with thoughts of like kind—opposing thoughts of a different character—forming combinations—going where they are attracted—flying away from thought centers opposing them. And your mind attracts the thoughts of others, which have been sent out by them consciously or unconsciously. But it attracts only those thoughts which are in harmony with its own. Like attracts like, and opposites repel opposites, in the world of thought.

If you set your mind to the keynote of courage, confidence, strength and success, you attract to yourself thoughts of like nature; people of like nature; things that fit in the mental tune. Your prevailing thought or mood determines that which is to be drawn toward you—picks out your mental bedfellow. You are to-day setting into motion thought currents which will in time attract toward you thoughts, people and conditions in harmony with the predominant note of your thought. Your thought will mingle with that of others of like nature and mind, and you will be attracted toward each other, and will surely come together with a common purpose sooner or later, unless one or the other of you should change the current of his thoughts.

Fall in with the operations of the Law. Make it a part of yourself. Get into its currents. Maintain your poise. Set your mind to the keynote of Courage, Confidence and Success. Get in touch with all the thoughts of that kind that are emanating every hour from hundreds of minds. Get the best that is to be had in the thought world. The best is there, so be satisfied with nothing less. Get into partnership with good minds. Get into the right vibrations. You must be tired of being tossed about by the operations of the Law—get into harmony with it.

The Mind Building-Child

By WILLIAM WALKER ATKINSON

A presentation of practical New Thought for use in rearing our little ones. Divided into six parts, as follows:

Part I. The Two-Edge Sword of Suggestion.

Showing how the child's mind and character are being formed by every moment spent in the presence of its parents, and how with children, as with adults, the Law of Suggestion operates *unintentionally* as intentionally. A consideration of influence to be exerted and Influences from which the child should be protected.

Part II. The Cultivation of Self-Reliance.

How to develop a moral and mental backbone in the child. A child's best inheritance—Experience and Self Help.

The development of individuality.

Part III. Practical Education.

Cultivating the powers of observation and memory—Quickening the powers of perception. Creating Interest. Following Nature's plan. Educating the child along the line of its individual tendencies.

Part IV. The Religion of Health.

The application of the laws of Health-thought In the regulation of a child's every-day life. Acquainting a child with the natural laws of Health. The formation of physical habits. Instructing in the art of breathing. Encouraging physical exercise. Teaching the ideal of Health. Instructing in mental imagery. The real religion of Health.

Part. V. A Working Faith.

What position shall parents take who have scruples about teaching their child dogmas, creeds and theology long since discarded in their own lives? No necessity for a New Thought "creed," but only instruction in certain fundamental truths. The idea of a first Cause. The Immanence of God. The bit of Spirit within. The unworthiness of Fear. The value of some good old-fashioned Mental Science instruction. The encouragement of Individual Expression.

Part VI. Prenatalism and Perfect Parenthood.

The training of the child begins before its birth. Parental thought. Not *more* children *but better ones*. The conditions which should surround the birth of a child. "Husbands' rights" too often husbands' wrongs. Higher ideals of fatherhood and motherhood. The supreme joy of parenthood. A child not only one's offspring but a fellow soul. The true relationship between parent and child.

A Book for Every Mother and Every Father—Present orto-Be!

Bound attractively in stiff covers, tulip-colored, with conventional cover design in brown. 80 pp.; clear large type, good paper.

Price Fifty Cents Postpaid LOUISE RADFORD WELLS, Manager

The Library Shelf, 1299 Farwell Avenue, Chicago IN BUSINESS AND EVERY DAY LIFE

By William Walker A t k I n o a

An Intensely practical book of instruction in the every-day application of the force latent in Man. It hag proven so valuable to the business-man that firms have ordered from us dozens of copies for distribution among their salesmen, recognizing the fact that an application of its principles *increased the earning capacity and commercial value of thetr employee.* A striking testimonial I

Equally valuable haa it proven,—as hundreds of letters received by us will testify,—in daily life, in the attainment of specific ambitions, in the control of domestic environment, the acquirement of mental habits or qualities, and in the development of that power we call "personal magnetism", either as a potent dynamic force or as the exercise of an agreeable attraction creating friends and smoothing difficulties.

Thousands of copies of this work have been sold. Why?

Because It la not theoretical,—It Is Intensely and simply practical.

Because It Is not mystical or Involved. It la clear, lucid "plain talk". Interesting, vivid, Inspiring, but always and ever UNDERSTANDABLE and applicable by the reader, be he novice or adept.

Because It answers such questions as theses

How can I attain material success? How can I affect my circumstances by mental effort? Just how shall I go about it to free myself from my depression, failure, timidity, weakness and care? How am I to recognize the causes of my failure and thus avoid them? Can I make my disposition into one which is active, positive, high strung and masterful? How can I draw vitality of mind and body from an invisible source? How can I directly attract friends and friendship? How can I influence other people by mental suggestion? How can I cure myself of illness, bad habits, nervousness? etc.

The titles of the chspters or "lessons" of which the book is composed, are as follows:

Lesson I, Salutatory: Lesson II, The Nature of The Force! Lesson III, How

Thought Force Can Aid Tou: Lesson IT, Direct Psychic Influence: Lesson V, A Little Worldly Wisdomt Lesson VI, The Power of the Eye: Lesson Til, The Magnetic Gaze: Lesson Tin, The Tolic Force: Lesson IX, Direct Volatlon: Lesson X, Telepathic Tulatlon: Lesson XI, The Adductive Quality of Thought: Lesson XII, Character Building by Mental Control: Lesson XIII, The Art of Concentrating: Lesson XIV, The Practice of Concentrating: Lesson XT, Valedictory.

Bach chapter has from 10 to 25 subtopics or headings. Here are the subheadings for Lesson XII, "Character Building by Mental Control": *Man can make of himself what he will—Regeneration no idle dream—A living truth—Strong facultiet made etronger, weak facultiee developed—The new "Regenerator"—The Law of Mental Control—The new path through the woode—Making yourself over— To breakup old thought haoite and form new onee—The four great methods—Force of Will—Hypnotic Suggestion— Auto-Suggestion—Thought Absorption—Ideal treatment—Full instructions in the theory of each of the four methods, showing their respective advantages and disadvantages, with illustrations of each—Bow to acquire a desired quality of mind—The practice of Thought Absorption—Practical exercises and directions—exercises 1 to t—Tou are your own master—Make of yourself what you will.*

The size of book is 6 by 9 inches. It is printed in clear, large type, on good paper, and contains 91 pages. It is bound in purple silk cloth with gold lettering. Price, $1.00 postpaid. Address, *THE LIBRARY SHELF 1299 FARWELL AVBNUB--CHICAQO, ILL., U. S. A.* THE LAW OF THE NEW

Tlinilout Fundamtntal Prln-I nUUUn I ciples and Their Application

By William Walker Atkinson

What Mr. Atkinson says about It:

"I consider this book is the best thing I have ever written. In It I have embodied the fundamental principles of The New Thought, as I understand them, in a plain, understandable form. I hare endeavored to make this a practical book and I feel that I have succeeded. It Is

no easy matter to present the highest truths—the fundamental principles—of The New Thought In words that may be understood by the many." "This book takes up the deep questions of Man—his relation to the Universe—his relation to the Supreme Power—his spiritual unfoldment and growth—his latent powers—his destiny—his possibilities. It tells of man's spiritual, mental and psychic powers and their development. It tells of the Something Within. It tells of the growth of consciousness— from mere sensation to Cosmic Knowing. It tells of the broader and greater concept of the Universal Presence—God. It tells of the manifestation of the Supreme Wisdom, Power and Presence. It tells of the Oneness of All—that key to the vexed questions of Life, Philosophy and Religion.

"I have not soared above the clouds In writing this book, bnt have kept my feet squarely on the ground. I have endeavored to deliver my message clearly and plainly. I do not hesitate to recommend this, my own book, to my friends who are Interested In this great subject. This may seem to Indicate that I am lacking In modesty, but I would use Just the same words If the book had been written by another." The titles of the chapters are as follows: What Is the New Thought?—Thoughts are Things—The Law of Attraction—Mind Building—The Dweller of The Threshold—Mind and Body —The Mind and Its Planes—The Sub-Conscious Plane—The Super-Conscious Faculties—The Soul's Question—The Absolute—The Oneness of All—The Immortality of The Soul—The Unfoldment—The Growth of Consciousness—The Soul's Awakening.

Each chapter contains a large number of sub-topics. Here are the sub-headings ot Chapter VIII: *The greater part of our thinking performed along sub-conscious lines—Illustrations of this fstc£—the sub-conscious, the habit plane—Means by which the sub-conscious menal'tity is reached—A storehouse of thoughts—A mixture of wisdom and foolish' ness—How the super-conscious faculties manifest first along sub-*

conscious tines—A reservoir receiving conscious thoughts—The desirability of a clear supplying stream —Auto Suggestions and affirmations—Did thought originate on the conscious, or sub conscious planet My views on the subject—Filling the storehouse with proper material—Creating on the thought plane—Our own thoughts, not others—Disease producing on the subconscious plans—Thoughts take form in action—As a man thinketh in his heart, so is he.

The book Is bound In purple silk cloth with gold lettering, Is 6 by 9 Inches, contains 93 pages and costs $1.00, postpaid. Address, THE LIBRARY SHELF 1299 FARWELL AVENUE CHICAGO, ILL, U. S. A.

i Nuggets of the New Thought

Several things that have helped people by William Walker Atkinson

A collection of some of the most famous writings of this famous author, Including his "SECRET OF THE I AM," of which almost 100,000 copies have been sold singly, his equally famous "I CAN AND I WILL," which is the keynote of New Thought philosophy, and his story of "JERRY AND THE BEAR," perhaps the most widely popular of all his essays, having been copied and recopied in magazines and publications of every class.

NUGGETS is perhaps the best "all-round" New Thought book published, having something for every mood and every stage of growth. It is good for the scoffer, good for the beginner, good for the adept. Men feel its practical inspiration—women treasure its deep and beautiful lessons. CONTENTS. 1. The Keynote. 2. The Secret of The I Am. 3. "Let A Little Sunshine In." 4. The Hunger of the Soul. 5. Look Aloft. 6. Tomorrow. 7. In The Depths of The Soul. 8. Forget It. 9. The Kindergarten of Qod. 10. The Human Wet Blanket. II. Aim Straight. 12. At Home. 13. The Solitude of The Soul. 14. Jerry and The Bear. 15. The Unseen Hand. 16. How Success Comes. 17. The Man With The Southern Exposure. 18. A Foreword. 19. Partnership. 20. The Seekers. 21. Mental Pictures. 22. Don't Retail Your Woes. 23. Life. 24. Let Us Have Faith. 25. Do It Now. 26. Get In Tune. 27. Mental Toxin and Anti-Toxin.

Each article has from ten to twelve subheadings. Here are those of: 1. THE KEYNOTE. "I Can And I Will"—The Recognition—Equal to any task—A feeling of calm confidence—An abiding sense of power—reserve force and security—The Something within—The triple key to the door of Attainment—The vibrations of Success.

2. THE SECRET OF THE I AM. The Ego—The physical plane—the mental plane—the new plane of consciousness—The Real Self—The "I"—The Temple of the Living Spirit—Development of the "1 Am" consciousness—The Higher Reason. 26. GOT IN TUNE. Marconi's wireless messages—Vibrations reach only the instruments attuned to the sender—The same law in operation on the mental plane—The correct pitch Is the thing—Get in tune with the proper vibrations— Get the messages from the best senders. 27. MENTAL TOXIN AND ANTI-TOXIN. A new toxin—The microbes In the thoughts we think—The new anti-toxin—Thoughts may poison—Fear causes paralysis—Hate causes insanity—Fear and Hate have killed their thousands —Gates' experiments—How to overcome the poison of bad-thinking.

The size of the book is 6x9 inches. It is printed in clear type on good paper, and contains 92 pages. It is bound in purple silk cloth with gold lettering. Price $1.00, postpaid. Address, THE LIBRARY SHELF 1299 Farwell Avenue:::: Chicago, Illinois SELF-HEALING BY THOUGHT FORGE

By WILLIAM WALKER ATKINSON

A Series of Lessons in Self-Healing: Practical — Plain — Powerful t

A HINT OF THE CONTENTS: FIRST LESSON: A consideration of the principles underlying healing by the power of the mind—The One Great Force back of Suggestive Therapeutics, Mental Science, Christian Science, Faith Cure, and all the rest—The patient the real healer—The innate recuperative power—How Nature works through the nerve currents—How lost functioning powers are stimulated—The blood is the life—Keeping the circulation normal—The law of reciprocity—The ability to generate and use mental reserve force, never lost—Improper thinking a mental brake—Mind manifesting on the physical plane—Calling into play the reserve stock of nerve power, nerve impulse or "Thought-Force"—Changing the circulation at will—Stimulating the nerve current by Thought-Force.

FIRST SELF-TREATMENT: For Equalizing the Circulation. Useful in any kind of case. Every self-treatment should begin with this Equalizing Treatment before treating the special organ affected. A Thorough lesson in method and procedure. SECON D LESSON: The main organs of nutrition—Indigestion, dyspepsia— How Man obtains his strength—The effect of mental influence on the appetite and digestive organs—Normal functioning of the organs of nutrition prime requisite for health—How to build up these organs—Sending increased nervecurrents to the affected parts—The use of Auto-Suggestion—The laying on of hands—Propelling a current of Thought-Force. SECOND SELF-TREATMENT: For Stomach troubles. Indigestion, Dyspepsia. A treatment in three divisions, with instructions for each. THIRD LESSON: Removal of clothing during treatment not absolutely necessary—Best time for treatment at night and in morning—The treatment of Constipation—The reason for this bowel condition—Shutting off the wrong thought current—Necessity of conforming to both mental ana physical law— The re-establishment of normal conditions—The important part of fluids in the human economy—How the body becomes like a dried apple—Forming a habit for the sphincter-ani muscle. THIRD SELF-TREATMENT: For Constipation. This treatment to be taken for establishing normal conditions of the bowels. "Cured by this method, you will stay cured." FOURTH LESSON: The special physical weaknesses of women—the subconscious mental powers—the great healing medium—The nerve current sent out from the great Dynamo, the brain—A run-down state of the system—How to overcome "female" conditions—Building up the general health—Increasing the functioning power of the main organs. FOURTH SELF-TREATMENT: Very comprehensive, covering several special and aggravating female conditions. Explicit and practical. FIFTH LESSON: The American Disease"—Nervousness—At the bottom of many disorders—Making use of the force within us—Getting rid of negative thought —Starting the machinery—Attending to the character of your thoughts—The value of the treatment for "equalizing the circulation" in all nervous conditions. FIFTH SELF-TREATMENT: For Nervousness. Insomnia and Sleeplessness cured. The simplicity of the treatment—The result of years of thought and investigation—Removing the cause. SIXTH LESSON: How to start out In self-treatments — No mystery or magic—Putting thought force back of everything—The force available to anyone —Don't attribute your cure to anybody's pet theory—Performing wonderful cures—Power the growth of confidence—The mental attitude of the patient— Treating a diseased organ as if it possessed intelligence—How to "get right down to business"—A rebellious organ gradually correcting itself under treatment. AN EPILOGUE: A resume of principles—Negative conditions—Attracting injurious influences—The vibrations of unhealth—Mental microbes—A final Health Thoughtl

The book has a mission to perform, as Is indicated by the hundreds of letters we receive monthly, asking for lust this kind of help. Bound attractively In Fairfield brlstol covers, tulip-colored, with conventional cover design in brown. 91 pp.; clear large type, good paper. PRICE, FIFTY CENTS.

Louise Radford Weill, Manager, THE LIBRARY SHELF, 1299 Farwell Avenue, Chicago iBi The Science of Observing, Remembering and Recalling-"m ` By WILLIAM WALKER ATKINSON

This work treats of a rational, natural, easily acquired system of developing the faculties of observation and memory, depending upon no tricks, catch words, "patent methods," etc., but proceeding to gradually develop the faculties Instead of loading down the memory with "methods." It points out the way by which the memory in general as well as the special memories of places, faces, names, dates, prices, etc., may be developed. This book also explains and gives Instruction in the great Hindu system of memorizing, whereby the Orientals memorize their acred teachings and philosophies. Numerous examples and anecdotes Illustrating the principles enunciated are given, and the lessons are accompanied with exercises calculated to materially strengthen and develop the mental faculties of observation, remembrance and recollection. ———

——————— CHAPTERS

The Subconscious Storehouse—Attention and Concentration—Acquiring Impressions—Eye Perception and Memory—Exercises in Eye Perception—Ear Perception and Memory—Exercises In Ear Perception—Association—Remembrance, Recollection and Recognition—General Principles Regarding Impressions—The Cumulative System of Memory Culture— The Ten-Question Thought System—Memory of Figures, Dates and Prices —Memory of Places—Memory of Faces—Memory of Names—Artificial Systems.

Silk Cloth, Purple and Gold. Price, 81.00 Postpaid

"""jiftasJ " The Library Shelf., gSJofi ATT.

THE MIND'S ATTAINMENT *Sksssa* URIEL BUCHANAN if known throughout the country as a writer and author of exceptional power, remarkable for the serenity of his philosophy, his even poise and the blending of the truly practical in his writings with the Spiritual, the Ideal, The object of this book is to make clear the path of mental, physical and material attainment through the power of the mind. In the writer's own words: *"Inherent in every mind are potentialities for reaching the highest goal of human attainment. Man shapes his environment and determines his place in the world in exact accord with the use he makes of interior forces. "The aim of this work is distinctly practical. It reveals some of the great laws which govern the workings of human thought. It points out the way how best to show forth the ideal, to materialize our dreams and yearnings in every-day life.* " THE CHAPTERS OF THE BOOK

The Supreme Force The Sovereign Will The Higher Life

Han's Divinity The Power of Silence Our Destiny

Mysteries Individual Supremacy Human Progress

The Science of Breath The Spirit of Youth Divine Guidance

Self-Mastery Mental Influences A Lesson from Nature

Mental Control Elements of Success Aspiration

The Law of Suggestion Demand and Supply The Highest Goal

The work la 6 Inches by 9 inches, bound in purple silk cloth with gold letter-CI nOstOclid inf. It contains 91 pages, and is printed in clear type on good paper. Price wsjs.jj»im : ADDRESS

A NEW BOOK FROM THE LIBRARY SHELF JUST OFF THE PRESS, DECEMBER 33rd.

OUR INVISIBLE SUPPLY: HOW TO OBTAIN By FRANCES LARIMER WARNER

The object of this book is to show how we may claim and receive what we all desire—money, success, companionship, fulfilled ambitions—what we will! The book consists of a series of personal letters from Mrs. Warner to her students (actual letters, thus reprinted), answering specific inquiries and perplexities and detailing methods of "obtaining."

Mrs. Warner's own personal experiences in demonstrating the Law of Supply, are frankly given, and as she has had very tangible obstacles to overcome—poverty, ill health, trouble, etc.—it is interesting to see how she has in fact and truth, obtained from "Our Invisible Supply," the things she needed or longed for.

The letters are not theoretical or abstruse, but clear, straightforward, real. Each is a distinct lesson in manifesting prosperity; and each analyzes some condition presented in letters from students (conditions very like to those of our own personal problems) and shows why failure exists, how it may be over-come, what methods to pursue, etc.

The book will prove, we think, about the oest-selling book of the season, be-cause so fully answering an almost uni-versal demand.

It is printed on excellent paper, with ornamental initial letters and tail pieces, large clear type; bound in light green cloth with cover bearing title in white, and facsimile signature of author, also in white. Not only a very attractive vol-ume, but one which will help YOU at-tract the prosperity you desire t PRICE, ONE DOLL4R LOUISE RADFORD WELLS, manager

The Library Shelf, 1299 Farwell Av-enue, Chicago

The Heart of the New Thought

▲ LOVABLE PHILOSOPHY OF SIM-PLEST CONSTRUCTION

By ELLA WHEELER WILCOX (*Writtm especially for The New Thought Pub-lishing Company. Mrs. Wilcox received many thousand dollars as pay-ment for this perfect work).*

Tills book has proved one of the greatest literary successes In the New Thought world. Thirty thousand copies were ordered as a first edition. In antic-ipation of an unusual demand, but be-fore the books were off the press It was necessary to Increase the order to fifty thousand, to meet the advance orders. The tremendous sales of The Heart of The New Thought are a witness both to the strong hold Ella Wheeler Wilcox deservedly has upon the heart of the American people, and to the high char-acter, the practical value, and "everyday helpfulness" of the book Itself. Mrs. Wilcox tells how to accomplish what she advocates. The book teaches The Power of Right Thought. "What Mrs. Wilcox says is practical, what she thinks is clear, what she feels Is plain."

Some of the subjects treated In the book are as follows!
(1) Let the Fast Go. (Bow to make a fresh start In life.) (2) The Sowing of the Seed. (A practical word to the begin-ner in New Thought.) (3) Old Clothes. (Showing how even,. small things may maintain a wrong thought-atmosphere.) (4) High Noon. (For women who have passed thirty—a heartto-heart talk.) (5) Obstacles. (How to overcome.) (6) Thought Force. (How to use the power of thought.) (7) Opulence. (What cre-ates and what overcomes Poverty con-ditions.) (8) Eternity. ("To be able to en Joy heaven, one must learn first to enjoy earth.") (9) Morning Influences. (How to strike the right keynote for the day. We have been repeatedly urged to print this chap-ter in pamphlet form.) (10) The Philosophy of Happiness. (How to acquire "the habit of happiness. ') (11) A Worn Out Creed. (The old thought vs. the new.) (12) Common Sense. (Flaws In health, habits, temper, disposition, and how to overcome them.) (18) Literature. (The value of right read-ing and thinking.) (14) Optimism. (The keynote of New Thought.) (15) Preparation. (How to ed-ucate oneself for a "charming old age.") (16) Dividends. (Thought Invest ments and what they pay.) (17) Royalty. (Our divine inher itance.) (18) Heredity. (A talk on self-crea tion.) (19) Invincibili-ty. (The Irresistible Desire-force and Its use.) (20) That Mental Chisel. (A talk on "face-build-ing.") (21) The Object of Life. (22) Wisdom. (How to rightly "de mand one's own.") (23) Self-Conquest. (The domination of physical and material conditions entirely possible, but not an Immediate process.) (24) The Important Trifles. (The small things often forgot-ten by the beginner In New Thought.) (25) Concentration. (How to ac quire the power.) (26) Destiny. (How to be master of your own.) (27) Sympathy. (Use and misuse.) (28) The Breath. (A lesson on deep breathing and Its value.) (29) Generosity. (The law of giving and its returns of prosperity.) (30) Woman's Opportunity. (A talk on Pre-natallsm.) (81) Balance. (Common-sense la New Thought.)

This hook Is printed on good paper. In large type, well-leaded, wide mar-gins, contains 92 pages, and is bound In purple silk cloth, with gold lettering. Size of the book, 6 by 9 Inches. Price, $1.00 postpaid. Address, 1299 FAR-WELL AVENUB -CHICAGO. ILL., U. S. A. THE LIBRARY SHELF.

The OccultewesAThe Mystic

This book is the first of our series of Psychic and Occult Books, and is called therefore, "Series A." The lessons con-tained therein were formerly included with several other courses in our book of Psychic Instruction, of which Mrs El-la Wheeler Wilcox writes: *"Iwas espe-cially interested in the first and last parts of your book of Psychic Instruc-tion. I have recommended these very highly."* The parts referred to are the ones comprised in Series A. They deal with Personal Force of Character, Suc-cess, Soul-Growth and Zoistn, the Divine Science.

Part I—A Course in Personal Mag-netism in 15 Lessons

A VERY FEW of the subjects touched upon are:

The Nature of Mental Currents—Ex-tracting Power from DesirePlenty of Force on Every Hand—The Method of Operation—Evidence of Strength In Desire-Force—Use Force from the Other Man—How to Use Antagonistic Forces for Your Own Benefit—Recog-nizing the Available Force—A Splen-did Exercise for Absorbing Energy—The Central Gane— The Magnetic Handshake—The Cultivation of the Magnetic Glance— The Mirror Exer-cise—Three Private Methods of Direct Radiation of the Magnetic Influence—(1) Mental Photography—(2) Solar-Plexus Method— (3) The Muscular Method—Methods of Active Projec-tion-Relation between Mental and Ma-terial—A Process of Induction—Pro-jecting Force Through Affirmation.

PART H—ZOISM: A Course of Instruc-tion in the Philosophy and Practice of the Higher Mental Science for the At-tainment of Health, Happiness and Spir-itual Peace.

A few of the subjects treated are:

Zone, the Life Energy—The Zone Manifest—Mind an Instrument— The Mind Manifest—The State of Super-consciousness—Illumination from the Soul—The Forces Acting upon the

Mind—The Practical Nature of Zoism-Wealth Is Attracted—Health Is Given—The Eight Commandments—The Keynote of Zoism—What the Practices are FiSr—The Present Relation of Mind and Body in You—The Process of Worry—What Control of Zone Means—The Importance of Retaining the Breath—The Full Breath—The Highest Function of The Mind—The Three Steps—The Practice of Attractive Concentration—The Five Objects-Directing the Subconscious—The Force of Assumption—The Compelling Force of Desire— The Developing Powers—The First Step in Pure Concentration—The Attainment of Superconsclousness—What this State is—How to Practice This—The Yisible Evidence of The Presence of the Soul—The Zolst—His Mission—His Power.

PRICB OF SBRIES A containing the above courses of Psychic lessons,

———————— ONLY 1.00 POSTPAID

This book is bound in purple silk cloth, with gold lettering, contains 96 pages, size 0x6 inches.

Write for particulars of our other Occult Books on Hypnotism, Magnetic Healing, Clairvoyance and Crystal Gazing, Personal Magnetism, Auto-Suggestion, Concentration, Mind-Reading, Psychometry, Phrenology, Palmistry, Astrology and Mediumship. i ADDRESS

——————— THE LIBRARY SHELF 1299 Farwell Avenue:::: CHICAGO, ILL., U. S.

A. PRICE 10 CENTS

A Dainty Little Booklet, containing:

Directions for 32 healthful, original and appetizing SALADS, 24 of which are delicious combinations of vegetables and fruits

Directions for 6 famous SALAD DRESSINGS.

Directions for 20 styles of dainty SANDWICHES, with varied fillings, including toothsome combinations of fruits, nuts, vegetables or meats.

Just the thing for the housewife who has learned that there is no quicker way to lessen her labor than by the plentiful use of.salads, and no food combination so effective in promoting proper functioning of the bowels, or so useful as a medium for introducing desirable tissue-building elements into the system.

A Booklet which would be particularly suggestive and useful to the woman undertaking to fill home-catering orders for picnics, parties, etc.

Prepared for and purchased by us from one of the largest food specialty houses in the country.

THE LIBRARY SHELF 1299 Farwell Avenue CHICAQO, ILL. HOW TO ENTERTAIN PRICE 10 CENTS

A little Booklet of Correct Ideas, Recipes and Suggestions telling How to Serve a Dinner, How to Serve a Luncheon, What to Serve at Afternoon Tea, What to Serve at Receptions, What to Serve at Card Parties.

Containing also 12 Ideas for Holiday Entertaining, including Easter, an April "Rainy-Day," May-day, Fourth of July, Thanksgiving, Halloween, Christmas,

Containing also directions for 7 Delicious "Relishes" for Dainty Refreshments, 8 Tested Recipes for Special Fruit Drinks.

8 Recipes for Salads Without Meat. 4 Original Recipes for Nut and Fruit Sandwiches. 6 Recipes for Appetizing Nut and Fruit Desserts. 3 Recipes for Frozen Desserts. 6 Recipes for Nut and Fruit Cakes. 6 Recipes for Delicious "Table Sweetmeats." 9 Recipes for Home-Made Confections (cooked). 6 Recipes for Home-Made Confections (without cooking).

This little booklet gives *direction about the arrangement of the table,* the order in which courses should be served, etc.

If you entertain, if you like dainty, original dishes, if you wish to be in a position to undertake to provide the refreshments for others who do entertain, you will find this little pamphlet full of pertinent and original suggestions.

THE LIBRARY SHELF 1299 Farwell Avenue CHICAQO, ILL. STANFORD UNIVERSITY LIBRARIES CECIL H. GREEN LIBRARY STANFORD, CALIFORNIA 94305-6004 (415) 723-1493

All books may be recalled after 7 days DATE DUE *i*

CPSIA information can be obtained at www.ICGtesting.com
Printed in the USA
LVOW110418101212

310865LV00004B/50/P